ORWELL'S GHOSTS

ORWELL'S GHOSTS

Wisdoms and Warnings for the Twenty-First Century

LAURA BEERS

W. W. NORTON & COMPANY
Independent Publishers Since 1923

To Gabe and Alex,
I agree with Orwell—kids are awful fun
in spite of the nuisance.

CONTENTS

Introduction: WHAT'S ORWELLIAN?   11

1. FROM ERIC BLAIR TO GEORGE ORWELL
   The Making of a Writer   23

2. THE THOUGHT POLICE
   Censorship, Cancel Culture, and "Fake News"   43

3. ISMS
   Populism and Tyranny   75

4. INEQUALITY
   Accents and Manners and the Cut of Clothes   99

5. PATRIARCHY
   The Vote, Equal Pay, and Reproductive Rights   129

6. BLUEPRINT FOR REVOLUTION
   Making the Case for Democratic Socialism   161

   AFTERWORD
   For Freedom's Sake   191

   Acknowledgments   207

   Notes   211

   Index   229

Introduction

WHAT'S ORWELLIAN?

We are living in an Orwellian moment, although not in the sense that many political and cultural commentators understand the term. In recent years, with the rise of "cancel culture," "fake news," and concerted disinformation campaigns, invocations of Orwell and his classic dystopian novel *Nineteen Eighty-Four* have reached new heights. Conservatives have accused both their governments and the mainstream media of carrying out an "Orwellian" campaign of information management. In the aftermath of the January 6, 2021, insurrection at the US Capitol, Republican Senator Josh Hawley compared the cancellation of his book contract to life in Orwell's *Nineteen Eighty-Four*. Right-wing critics branded President Biden's now defunct Disinformation Governance Board within the Department of Homeland Security as a new "Ministry of Truth" in 2022. And, in June 2023, Supreme Court Justices Neil Gorsuch and Sonia Sotomayor argued over whether a Colorado public accommodations law that would compel a web designer to create a wedding website for a gay couple could be construed as "Orwellian thought policing" in their majority and dissenting opinions in *303 Creative LLC v. Elenis.*

The left, too, has embraced the rhetoric of Orwellianism, turning the term against former US president Donald Trump, as in Adam Gopnik's 2017 *New Yorker* essay, "Orwell's '1984' and Trump's America," and against former British prime minister Boris Johnson, as when Rafael Behr denounced Johnson's last Queen's speech as "inane and Orwellian" in a column in the *Guardian.* Outside the Anglosphere, the populist former Brazilian president Jair Bolsonaro's approach to information management was frequently denounced as "Orwellian," particularly in reference to his seeming determination to censor evidence of deforestation in the Amazon. Most recently, the term has been wielded against Russian president Vladimir Putin's attempts to manage information on the Ukraine war.

Given the amount of Orwell in the ether these days, it is unsurprising that *Nineteen Eighty-Four* has ranked in or near the top hundred books sold on both US and British Amazon for the past several years and has held on to a top spot on the American Booksellers Association's Indie Bestsellers list. At the time of writing, the French translation was among the five hundred best-selling titles on Amazon.fr, the Portuguese translation ranked 181st on Amazon's Brazilian site, and a Russian translation was named the top-selling Russian ebook of 2022, a phenomenon that will be discussed further below. Seventy-five years after the book's near-simultaneous release in London and New York in June 1949, it seemingly remains as relevant as ever.

NINETEEN EIGHTY-FOUR IS A PROPHETIC INDICTMENT OF THE RISK to liberty posed by totalitarianism, but George Orwell is more than just his most famous novel. For those who have never read Orwell, or who have only read *Animal Farm* or *Nineteen Eighty-Four*, and even then perhaps not since they were young, the notion that Orwell's work has much to offer for thinking about either socialism or racial politics might initially seem bizarre. But Orwell was a broad and deep thinker who opposed inequality as fervently as he opposed censorship and tyranny.

Further, when he denounced tyranny and repression, he was not only pointing a finger at Stalin's Russia. Even as the shadow of the Soviet Union looms behind his two most famous novels, they are equally informed by Orwell's long-standing opposition to both British imperialism and European fascism. They are, in that sense, as much products of the 1920s and the 1930s as of the Cold War, and thus are simultaneously critiques of Stalinism and indictments of authoritarianism in all its forms. What they are not is condemnations of socialism. In fact, he openly professed to being a democratic socialist, and supported Clement Attlee's post-1945 Labour government in Britain. The question that bedeviled Orwell for the final dozen years of his life was whether and how a socialist society could be achieved that offered its citizens economic security and social equality without devolving into authoritarianism. Nowhere is this clearer than in his brief 1940 work *The Lion and the Unicorn*, which I discuss in chapter 6.

To his friends and literary contemporaries, Orwell's sense of social justice was his most outstanding characteristic. In the nearly seventy-five years since his death, the complexity of his political thought has been ironed out and replaced by a two-dimensional caricature of Orwell as an anti-totalitarian prophet. It's a caricature that obscures much of the nuance that renders his writing worthy of rereading today. In four book-length works of reportage and reflection, and a series of novels including *Burmese Days*, *Coming Up for Air*, *Animal Farm* and *Nineteen Eighty-Four*, as well as in countless essays for the British and international press, Orwell struggled to make sense of the chaos around him, or at least to chronicle that chaos with his trademark commitment to truth and plain speaking. Both his libertarian and his communitarian values are evident in his writing on issues ranging from racial and class dynamics in the British Empire to working-class housing in Wigan, England, to Republican politics in Spain. The one blind spot that marks out Orwell's writing was his inability to appreciate the negative impact of patriarchal structures on inter-war women. Orwell was a socialist, but decidedly not a feminist. In this sense, alas, he is not dissimilar to too many contemporary leftists, who continue to privilege class and racial struggles above gender equality.

———

WHILE THE PAST REMAINS A FOREIGN COUNTRY, THE UNCANNY parallels between the interwar decades and our present political moment give Orwell's writing a renewed salience in the twenty-first century. As in our own time, rising consumerism coupled with economic instability and soaring inequality; disenchantment with liberal democracy and the rise of totalitarianism; and the challenge to traditional social hierarchies presented by both feminism and anti-colonialism rendered the decades between the two world wars a period of immense uncertainty and upheaval. Ever since Orwell's death on January 21, 1950, politicians, scholars, and pundits have reveled in asking, "What would Orwell think?" about current events. This book does not attempt to answer that question, not least because George Orwell was a notoriously mercurial writer who not infrequently changed his political opinions as his own understanding of events shifted.

Instead of asking, "What would Orwell think?" the following chapters take Orwell's writing on the interwar decades as a lens through which to re-examine the crisis of our own historical moment. Historians, myself included, tend to be strong believers that understanding our past is crucial to making sense of our present. Orwell's writing represents an exceptional effort by an observer of and participant in the global upheavals of the 1920s through the 1940s to document and make sense of the world around him. He devoted his career to exposing the social injustices and political perversions of his era and asking his readers to face those truths. He was a child of the British Empire who grew to be a self-professed anti-imperialist and democratic socialist and a vocal critic of totalitarianism, perpetrated by both the left and right. His greatest strength as an author was arguably what he called his "power of facing unpleasant facts." It's a strength in short supply today. The following chapters will revisit Orwell's writing on truth and disinformation in politics; economic, racial, and gender inequalities; the appeal of and threat posed by political authoritarianism; and the promise offered by socialism, with the dual aims of gaining a deeper understanding of Orwell's politics and considering how we can use Orwell's writing on the interwar decades to gain a clearer understanding of our own political moment.

BECAUSE ORWELL'S ENDURING FAME AS A WRITER AND THINKER IS principally predicated on the critique of authoritarianism and the emphasis on the importance of propaganda and disinformation manifest in his final two novels, the term "Orwellian," even as defined by *Merriam-Webster*, relates specifically to the dystopia depicted in *Nineteen Eighty-Four*. That work has been translated into at least sixty-five languages, while *Animal Farm* has been translated into more than seventy. There have been two film adaptations of *Nineteen Eighty-Four*, two televised adaptations, as well as a stage adaptation that ran in London's West End from 2014–16 and had a limited run on Broadway in 2017. *Animal Farm* was made into a popular cartoon in 1954, which is still shown to schoolchildren today. (Given Orwell's brief stint as a film and theater critic during the Second World War, these adaptations would likely have gratified him.) In a recent study, the literary scholar John Rodden makes a distinction between Orwell the man and "Orwell" the cultural product, which offers a valuable lens for considering how both Orwell and his books have been repeatedly reappropriated for various political ends. This transformation had already begun before his early death from tuberculosis at age forty-six. Notably, while his first wife, Eileen O'Shaughnessy, had become Eileen Blair, his second wife, Sonia Brownell, took the surname Orwell when they married on October 13, 1949, in University College Hospital, where he was then an invalid. Sonia knew that she was marrying the myth, not the man, who was clearly not long for this world and who had premised his offer of marriage by saying that she would soon become the widow of a famous author.

In a sense, *Orwell's Ghosts* is yet another reappropriation, using

Orwell's writing on the early twentieth century to help us better understand our current political moment. Yet, the book aims to be true to the author's original intent. It focuses tightly on his writing, drawing on the language of his novels, essays, and long-form journalism to elaborate a picture of the world as he understood it. Rather than imposing my twenty-first-century worldview on Orwell, I've sought to ask how understanding Orwell's own worldview can offer new ways of thinking about the present day.

WITH THE DEFEAT OF FASCISM, SUCCESSFUL DECOLONIZATION campaigns, and the collapse of communism between 1989 and 1991, liberal democracy briefly appeared to have triumphed over authoritarianism at the turn of the last century. In the past decade, however, history appears to have caught back up with us. Liberal democracy is once again on shaky ground, under threat from critics across the political spectrum and unable to secure its promised benefits for people of color, women, and other underrepresented groups. Critics on both the left and right are once again calling for social revolution, or, at the least, better regulation and reform of global capitalism. On the right, these critiques take the form of xenophobic anti-immigrant policies and calls for protective tariffs. The left, in turn, has sought to tame capitalism through greater worker protections and environmental regulation. But in countries such as Britain and the United States, even modest calls for reform from politicians such as Keir Starmer and Joe Biden are struggling to achieve a critical mass of support. The perceived failures of the existing system, combined with the lack of support for progressive reform and the rise of antidemocratic demagoguery designed to appeal to capitalism's losers, is again forcing us to confront the question that bedeviled Orwell: Can a socialist revolution be achieved democratically, without the sacrifice of liberty?

―――――

THE CHAPTERS THAT FOLLOW DO NOT PRESUPPOSE THE READER'S familiarity with Orwell's oeuvre or his life story. Rather, they are written to be accessible to those who haven't read Orwell since being assigned *Animal Farm* in middle school or *Nineteen Eighty-Four* in high school or college. Or, for that matter, those who have not read Orwell at all, but who are familiar with the term *Orwellian* and curious to learn more about its origin and meaning. I was inspired to write this book after several years of teaching a seminar at American University on George Orwell and the Making of the Modern World. At the beginning of each class, I ask students how much familiarity they have with Orwell's writing. Few have read more than his two famous novels, with the occasional student having read the essay "Shooting an Elephant" about Orwell's experience as a police officer in Burma, or his memoir of the Spanish Civil War, *Homage to Catalonia*. Many come to the class having never read Orwell at all. By the end of the semester, they are invariably firm believers in the enduring value of Orwell's writing for understanding both our past and our present.

As someone who loves to reread Orwell—even when I disagree with him—I am hopeful that, whatever level of familiarity with his writing you bring to this book, you'll leave determined to pick up one of his novels or a book of his essays and dive deeper into his work. Not least because Orwell is one of the few writers who never fails to make me laugh—usually to make me guffaw. In addition to his published writing, his private letters, now available in numerous edited collections, are a treat. He was a great lover of lists, and is often funniest when he is enumerating, as when he compiles a list of five rules for writing clear English and then appends a sixth, "Break any of these rules sooner than say anything outright barbarous," or when he compiles a short list of people unable to appreciate the changing of the seasons: "Spring is here, even in London N.1, and they can't stop you enjoying it. . . . So long as you are not actually ill, hungry, frightened or immured in a holiday camp, spring is still spring." Even when his writing is completely apolitical, it remains worth revisiting; but his political writing is characterized by an insight and honesty that marks it as some of the best in the English language.

ORWELL'S GHOSTS

1

FROM ERIC BLAIR TO GEORGE ORWELL

The Making of a Writer

Born on June 25, 1903, in Motihari, Eric Arthur Blair did not adopt the pen name George Orwell until the publication of his first published book, *Down and Out in Paris and London*, in 1933, and never legally changed his name. His father, Richard (Dick) Walmesley Blair, was a comparatively modest imperial administrator—an assistant sub-deputy agent, later promoted to sub-deputy. He was tasked with overseeing the production of opium in India for export to China, whose ports had been opened to the highly addictive substance in the Opium Wars of the mid-nineteenth century. While officially a member of the Imperial Civil Service, with all of the respect and social standing that went with the post, Richard was in effect a mid-level drug dealer, overseeing the production of an extractive cash crop, the dependency on which impoverished both the Indian producer and the Chinese consumer while directing immense profits to the British middlemen who handled the opium trade.

Eric's father was not the only problematic imperial skeleton
in the Blair closet. His great-great-grandfather Charles Blair
built a fortune in Jamaican sugar cane on the back of slave labor.
With wealth came social cachet and marriage to Mary Fane, the
daughter of the eighth Earl of Westmorland. When the British
government abolished slavery in 1833, Charles Blair's son received
substantial financial compensation from the British state as "reparation" for the loss of nearly four hundred slaves on two Jamaican plantations. Over the generations that followed, the ill-gotten
gains of slavery were spread increasingly thin, such that Eric's
father, the youngest of ten children, was forced to earn his own
income. Yet, if the money was largely gone, the social cachet of
being descended from an earl remained. The Blair family treasured a portrait of Fane, which Eric would later inherit. (Orwell's
first wife, Eileen, who came from a wealthier but less storied family, wrote to a friend shortly after the couple married, mocking
the portrait and the family's pretensions: "the [Blair] house is
very small & furnished almost entirely with paintings of ances-
tors. . . . [One ancestor] went so grand that he spent all the money
& couldn't make more because slaves had gone out . . . [so now]
they are all quite penniless but still on the shivering verge of gentility as Eric calls it.")

Orwell's mother, Ida Limouzin Blair, came from a less socially
exalted, if also well-established imperial family, of French ances-
try. Ida's grandfather G. E. Limouzin was a shipbuilder and teak
merchant based in Moulmein in Burma (now Mawlamyine,
Myanmar), a large trading outpost of the British Raj. His son
Frank married an English woman, and the couple had nine children, including Ida, born in 1875, eighteen years after Richard
Blair. While born in Britain, Ida and her siblings were raised in

Burma, in an opulent household befitting their family's economic
and social position. Frank Limouzin, however, could not hold on
to the fortune that his father had built, and as a young woman Ida
went to work as a governess in India, where she met and married
the nearly forty-year-old Richard Blair in 1896, on the rebound
from a love affair with a man closer to her own age.

Ida and Richard's first child, Marjorie, was born in Ben-
gal province in 1898. Five years later, Ida gave birth to Eric. The
family had relocated north to Motihari by then. Richard's mid-
grade administrative career was characterized by frequent moves
around the empire, as his son's brief imperial career would be as
well. Ida, Marjorie and Eric, but not Richard, returned "home" to
England, specifically to Henley in Oxfordshire, when Eric turned
one. He retained no memories of India, although he grew up in a
household surrounded by mementos of his parents' time abroad.
In his 1939 novel *Coming Up for Air,* he offers up a nasty caricature
of the Anglo-Indian household in which he was raised:

> It's almost impossible, when you get inside these people's
> houses, to remember that out in the street it's England and
> the twentieth century. As soon as you set foot inside the
> front door you're in India in the [1880s]. . . . The carved teak
> furniture, the brass trays, the dusty tiger-skulls on the wall,
> the Trichinopoly cigars, the red-hot pickles, the yellow pho-
> tographs of chaps in sun-helmets, . . . the everlasting anec-
> dotes about tiger-shoots and what Smith said to Jones in
> Poona in '87.

Richard retired from the Indian Civil Service in 1912 on a comfortable pension of 438 pounds, ten shillings per annum and

returned to Britain to live out his retirement with his family, which now included a third child, Avril, conceived during his brief leave home from India in 1907.

A PSYCHIATRIST WOULD DOUBTLESS HAVE MUCH TO SAY ABOUT the fact that, as an adult, Orwell exhibited casual misogyny toward women, given that he was raised, until the age of nine, in an almost entirely female and apparently feminist environment. At home, he had his mother and sister (later sisters) and the non-live-in domestic help. The children attended an Anglican convent school in Henley from age five to eleven, where Eric was one of only a few male pupils, taught exclusively by women. Possibly his embrace of patriarchy was in part a reaction to his mother's feminism. His childhood friend Jacintha Buddicom, whom he met at age eleven, recalls that Eric told her that "one or two of [his Limouzin] aunts and their friends were Militant Suffragettes. Mrs Blair was in sympathy, but not so active. *Some* of this contingent, Eric said, went to prison and on hunger-strike as well as more moderately chaining themselves to railings."

In Shiplake, a small village outside of Henley, they had a bigger house and live-in help and Eric befriended both Jacintha and her brother Prosper, who became holiday friends, since Eric was now sent away to prep school. It says a lot about the Blair family's priorities that a very substantial proportion of their income went to expensively educating their children—all were sent to board at prep schools, although only Eric continued his education until he was eighteen.

Eric was a bright and bookish child. He read voraciously, particularly liked Kipling, Shakespeare, H. G. Wells, and Arthur

Conan Doyle. (As a teenager, he wrote at least one murder mystery of his own, and later in life declared himself an "*amateur* of detective stories," albeit one with "old fashioned tastes.") He both read and composed poetry. Although he showed symptoms of respiratory weakness, he was by no means an invalid. He fished, shot rifles, and played games, and did the things most normal Edwardian boys did for fun, but his bookishness stood him in good stead when his family put him forth for a scholarship, which he received, to St. Cyprian's.

St. Cyprian's was a prep school of relatively recent vintage, having been founded in 1899 in Eastbourne on the Sussex Downs. Most of the (all male) pupils' parents paid steep fees for their sons to attend the school, but Orwell's scholarship reduced the cost of his education from £180 to £90 per annum—still well in excess of the average male wage of roughly £50 per annum. Whether his parents would have paid the full fee for St. Cyprian's remains an open question. Certainly, they could have done so, although likely not without sacrificing Marjorie's education.

Eric excelled academically at St. Cyprian's, and forged what would be a lifelong friendship with another future Etonian and author, Cyril Connolly. Yet, in his later years, Orwell claimed to have loathed his time at the school. Shortly before his death, he penned "Such, Such Were the Joys," a vitriolic portrait of his time there that, owing to the risk of a libel suit from the school's owners, was not published in Britain until after their deaths. Connolly and other graduates have insisted that Orwell's colorful catalog of grievances was exaggerated. (These ranged from the unsanitary and disgusting, including the alleged sighting of a "human turd" floating in the local baths that the school boys frequented, to the barbarous, as when he claimed that the headmaster beat him for five minutes until his riding crop snapped. He was punished for daring to claim that a first, shorter beating had not hurt.) Jacintha Buddicom averred that he never let on that he hated the school so intensely. But, while his memories of his time at St. Cyprian's may have been tainted by hindsight, the one thing that comes through clearly in Orwell's essay and other references to his childhood is that St. Cyprian's was a place where money mattered, and where not having money—or at least having less money than many of your super-rich classmates—was a major social handicap.

Eric seemed to perceive his comparative socioeconomic position more as a personal affront than as a reflection of a fatally flawed system in which distinctions of class and status were given an outsized social weight. As a boy, he was a snob, but the snobbery "filled me with resentment against the boys whose parents were richer than mine and who took care to let me know it." As an adult, he self-consciously tried to repudiate the ingrained prejudices inherited from his childhood. One of the most famous passages from his 1937 social investigation and commentary *The Road to Wigan Pier* is his discussion of both the importance and the difficulty of unlearning the lesson taught to all middle-class children in childhood that "*the lower classes smell.*"

In 1917, Eric won a place as a King's Scholar at Eton, the illustrious prep school founded by Henry VI in 1440. His belated admission to the school likely hinged on one of the existing cohort of scholars enlisting in the First World War. While the conflict was ongoing, young Blair supported it unreservedly, even publishing two poems commemorating the war effort, although he later asserted that he and the other Eton boys had all become a bit " 'Bolshie,' as people then called it" by the end of the war. Orwell's first biographer, Peter Stansky, has recently argued for the underestimated importance of the First World War in cementing Orwell's sense of patriotism. Certainly, even when Orwell was at his most cynical about his country's capitalist system of class exploitation masked as parliamentary democracy, he never abandoned his patriotic love for England, embodied in the title of his 1940 essay "My Country Right or Left," in which Orwell seeks to reconcile his revolutionary socialist politics with his self-realization "that the long drilling in patriotism which the middle classes go through had done its work, and that once England was in a serious jam it would be impossible for me to sabotage."

As with England, so with Eton, it appears. Contemporaries remember Eric as somewhat aloof, not a joiner, but at the same time, not notably unhappy. While the adult Orwell regularly derided Eton as "a snobbish expensive public school" and one of the "festering centres of snobbery" that has kept Britain back, he nonetheless originally considered sending his adopted son, Richard, there. Many of his closest friends throughout his literary career were Old Etonians. Orwell once penned a scathing portrait of the "socialist intellectual" as an "Old Etonian" who "still leaves his bottom waistcoat button undone. . . . Perhaps once, out of sheer bravado, he has smoked a cigar with the band on, but it would be almost physically impossible for him to put pieces of cheese into his mouth on the point of his knife, . . . or even to drink his tea out of the saucer." Orwell was able to write with insight about such prejudices because he shared them, and, at the end of the day, despite having a few working-class friends like the felicitously named author Jack Common, he seems to have found it easier to relax with companions of his own sort.

Much ink has been spilled over the decades over the question of why Orwell did not go to Oxford or Cambridge like the rest of his class of King's Scholars, including his childhood friend Cyril Connolly. Some have suggested that he had not done well enough at Eton to secure a scholarship (certainly, this was the message that his tutor Andrew Gow gave him and his father), or that his family could not have afforded to pay his tuition. It is true that he had slacked off at Eton, but the mere fact of having been a King's Scholar would probably have been enough to get him an Oxford or Cambridge scholarship, had he tried for one. And, given the amount that they had poured into his education already, his family probably could have found the money for the fees.

Yet, they may well not have found it necessary. In 1921, when Eric finished school, universities were not the gateways to professional success that they are today. As late as 1951, when Winston Churchill (who himself had not been to university) was returned to Number 10 Downing Street, only fifty-two percent of the MPs elected to Parliament held university degrees. At just shy of nineteen, Eric might also have felt a restless desire to stop studying and start living. Writing of the 1920s from the vantage of 1940, Orwell recalled, "As the war fell back into the past, my particular generation, those who had been 'just too young', became conscious of the vastness of the experience they had missed. You felt yourself a little less than a man, because you had missed it."

His decision to enlist in the Indian Police Service in Burma most likely reflected a desire to stop studying and start *doing*. To leave his boyhood behind and become a man. His sense that his graduation from Eton represented a maturation into adulthood was also tragically manifested in his attempt to advance his relationship with Jacintha Buddicom. While the two families spent time together over the summer holiday before his final term at school, he suddenly made a move on his old friend during a country ramble—what one of his biographers classed as his character-istic "pounce." To Jacintha, his uninvited overture was not only unwelcome but threatening. She felt that Eric had assaulted her, and the incident put a permanent end to their friendship, some-thing Eric did not understand at the time. On his first leave back from Burma, he had intended to propose marriage to Jacintha, which would have been the first of his many unsuccessful propos-als of matrimony. Instead, she refused to see him, and the two never met again, although they briefly resumed a correspondence before his death.

Over the decades, Orwell scholars have ruminated on the impact of the botched seduction, suggesting, rather implausibly, that it accounted for his decision to join the IPS and seeing reflec-tions of Jacintha in several of the female characters with whom Orwell's (anti-)heroes have impromptu outdoor assignations in his novels. What is clear is that the experience of being soundly rebuffed and permanently defriended by Jacintha did not teach Blair/Orwell to respect women's boundaries and bodily autonomy.

If he didn't go to Burma because he was jilted by Jacintha, he may well have gone out of curiosity about the "outlandish place" where his mother was raised and where he still had family. The IPS had given him a choice of where within the vast British Raj he wanted to be sent. As to why he joined the IPS at all, it's quite plau-sible that his calculation was not that different than his father's. A man bred to social dominance but without vast financial means could live like a king in the Raj, as opposed to existing like a mem-ber of the lower-upper-middle class at home. It's clear that he was bothered by his comparative penury while at school, and Burma was a chance to live a better, or at least a more exalted, life, as his parents must have impressed on him throughout his childhood.

BUT RATHER THAN SETTLING INTO THE DESULTORY, SELF-SATISFIED existence of a *pukka sahib*, Blair's experience of imperial dominance in Burma awakened his social conscience and attuned him to identify and criticize oppression, not only within the empire, but at home in Britain, and abroad in the totalitarian regimes that were emerging to challenge liberal democracy from the left and the right. His time in Burma also cemented his determination to pursue a literary career. His transformation from aloof schoolboy to the "wintry conscience of a generation"—as his friend V. S. Pritchett dubbed him—began in the tropical heat of Burma.

IN 1927, AFTER FIVE YEARS OF SERVICE IN OUTPOSTS AROUND Burma, including in Moulmein, where his mother had grown up, Blair resigned from the IPS. He did not quit the police in a dramatic show of principle, despite the fact that, as he later wrote, he had come to hate the service by that point:

> I hated the imperialism I was serving with a bitterness which
> I probably cannot make clear. In the free air of England that
> kind of thing is not fully intelligible. In order to hate imperi-
> alism you have got to be part of it. Seen from the outside the
> British rule in India appears—indeed, it *is*—benevolent and
> even necessary. . . . But it is not possible to be a part of such
> a system without recognizing it as an unjustifiable tyranny.

Instead, he appears to have kept his loathing to himself, like the character John Flory in his first novel, *Burmese Days*, a lonely timber merchant who secretly hates the empire that provides his livelihood. Like Flory, he drowned his self-disgust in women and drink, while making an exceptional, if ultimately superficial, effort to learn about native language and culture.

Yet, while Flory is clearly a largely autobiographical character, Orwell was unable to invest the young British merchant with the full complexity of feelings he experienced as a policeman. As a sub-divisional police officer, stationed in various communities from the Irrawaddy Delta to the outskirts of Rangoon to his maternal family's hometown of Moulmein, he was tasked with disciplin-ing communities of tens of thousands of native Burmese who, for their part, felt his very presence in their country as a crime—a feeling that he came to share. Orwell paints the otherwise unap-pealing character of Westfield, the district superintendent of police in *Burmese Days*, with some of the shame and animosity that he felt about the practice of punishing the wretched. After a scene in which Westfield's Burmese subordinates condemn a gray, half-naked, "tick-bittened" coolie with a "timorous face" of hav-ing stolen an emerald ring based on nothing but class prejudice and circumstantial evidence, Westfield growls in self-disgust, "All right, put him in the clink." "At the bottom of his heart he loathed running in these poor devils of common thieves. Dacoits [armed robbers], rebels—yes; but not these poor cringing rats!"

The same sentiment of having been involved in something sor-did pervades his 1931 essay "A Hanging," in which he describes witnessing the execution of a poor, "puny wisp of a man, with a shaven head and vague liquid eyes," for a crime which is so irrel-evant as not to merit mention. He later claimed that the spectacle was "worse than a thousand murders." The essay ends with the officials—British and Burmans alike—laughing uncomfortably and drowning their discomfort in a bottle of whiskey. Five years

of enforcing the law in Burma left Blair unable to enter a jail without feeling that his "place was on the other side of the bars."

Yet, instead of resigning in protest, Blair requested a medical
leave of absence, and then, while safely home in England, put in
his resignation. In a sign of both his integrity and the extent of
his disillusionment with the IPS, he declined to draw his salary
for the duration of his medical leave, despite the fact that he had
limited savings and no imminent job prospects there. In fact, he
didn't remain in England long, perhaps finding it difficult to con-
template a return to life under his parents' roof after five years of
independence, servants, and concubines in Burma.

Only a few months after returning to England, Blair decamped
for Paris, where his aunt Nellie Limouzin lived a bohemian life
with her lover and later husband Eugene Adam, a devotee of the
Esperanto movement. Little is known about his time in Paris
other than what he subsequently chose to reveal in *Down and Out
in Paris and London* (1933) and in essays such as "How the Poor
Die," based on his experience being treated for pneumonia in the
public ward of a French hospital.

Down and Out was the first work published under Blair's pen
name, a composite of the name of England's patron saint and the
River Orwell, which flowed not far from where his parents and
younger sister were then living in Southwold, on the Suffolk coast.
Before it appeared, he had published a few short articles under
his own name. He chose to use a pen name principally to spare
his parents and sisters from embarrassment, as the book was in
essence a fictionalized retelling of his experience "slumming it"
with the poor of Europe's two great imperial capitals.

The first half of the book is effectively a stylized memoir of
his personal failures, tracing his experiences working various odd

jobs as he tried and struggled to make it as a writer. The second half, written after he moved back into his parents' house in Southwold in December 1929, is more contrived. Over the next several years, between romancing local women—at least one of whom, Mabel Fierz, was married, while another, Eleanor Jaques, was engaged to his old school friend Dennis Collings—Orwell made several brief trips to London during which he disguised himself and "went native" in the East End as social research for the second half of the book.

Despite his later protestations, there is no indication that Orwell set out to fail during his brief time in Paris. Rather, his experience of failure and destitution taught him the valuable lesson that poverty is not synonymous with moral degeneracy. This realization—not widely shared in 1920s Britain, a country still imbued with the Victorian ethos that the poor were poor as a consequence of their own moral failings—combined with his recognition that imperialism was, at its heart, exploitative to turn Orwell into a committed social critic. He did not at this point see himself as a socialist. He appears to have remained ignorant of socialist theory and to have paid little attention to the Russian Revolution. (His principal friend in Paris was a White Russian émigré, who would not have given him a good report of the Bolsheviks.) He was perhaps closest at this point to being, as his sister Avril would later brand him, a "Tory anarchist." He opposed the capitalist imperial order, but he remained at heart a traditionalist, imbued with the patriotic values of his childhood and implacably wedded to a patriarchal view of society.

Despite his not yet being a socialist, he was ultimately able to secure a contract for *Down and Out* with a socialist publisher, Victor Gollancz, who would play a major role in Orwell's literary development. The work only had an initial print run of 1,500, but garnered solid reviews in the major literary magazines and secured the newly christened George Orwell a livelihood that would allow him to finally move out of his parents' house in Southwold.

———

IN LONDON, ORWELL RENTED A FLAT IN HAMPSTEAD, DEVELOPED a profitable relationship with Richard Rees, then editor of the *New Adelphi*, for which he wrote regularly throughout the 1930s, published a good deal of fiction and nonfiction, and continued his pursuit of sex and romance, sometimes together, and sometimes distinct from one another. For the next several years, friends continued to know him as Eric, although he published principally as Orwell. By the end of the decade, however, the distinction between his personal and professional identities had blurred and friends increasingly knew him as George, and he often signed not only his professional writing but his personal correspondence with his adopted name. As George Orwell, he published four novels. He wrote *Burmese Days* in Paris, but could not find a publisher in the 1920s. Victor Gollancz ultimately brought out the book in the UK after publishing *Down and Out*. Gollancz also published his three subsequent novels, *A Clergyman's Daughter* (1935), *Keep the Aspidistra Flying* (1936), and *Coming Up for Air* (1939).

Unlike his nonfiction work in the 1930s, his novels are not explicitly political, although *Burmese Days* is a clear indictment of the empire. Cyril Connolly, who had not realized it was written by his old friend, described it in the *New Statesman* as a "crisp, fierce, and almost boisterous attack on the Anglo-Indian." *Coming Up for Air* is an implicit critique of the backward-looking quietism of many in the 1930s who failed to recognize the threat of fascism until it was too late—a quietism that Orwell could not endorse, despite his admiration for the author Henry Miller, whom he presents in his 1940 essay "Inside the Whale" as the ultimate quietist.

In 1936, Gollancz offered Orwell an advance to travel to the north of England and document the lives of the industrial working classes—both those still working and those suffering from long-term unemployment that, for many, dated back before the collapse of the New York Stock Exchange in October 1929, which set the Great Depression in motion. Across the north of England, an economic "slump" that began in the early 1920s had left a generation of young men living on the "dole"—the meager unemployment benefit offered by the state-run Public Assistance Committee.

Gollancz loved the first part of the resulting book, *The Road to Wigan Pier,* for its visceral, compassionate depiction of the plight of the northern poor. He was less enthusiastic about the second part, a classic example of Orwell's commitment to intellectual honesty, in which Orwell offered a sincere, and at times highly unflattering, assessment of how he had come to see himself as a socialist. He had decided that he was in sympathy with socialism and opposed to capitalism as an iniquitous system little better than fascism. He had also decided that most British socialists were intolerable "cranks," and said that as well. Given that Gollancz had decided to publish *Road to Wigan Pier* as a selection for his Left Book Club, whose forty thousand subscribers included many principally socialist intellectuals, he was unsurprisingly irritated with Orwell's use of that term. In the end, he published it with minimal amendment, although he appended his own foreword, which made clear that the second section of the book reflected Orwell's views and not those of the series publisher and that, indeed, "the whole of this second part is highly provocative, not merely in its general argument, but also in detail after detail. I had, in point of fact, marked well over a hundred minor passages about which I thought I should like to argue with Mr. Orwell."

With Orwell's newfound commitment to socialism—however unorthodoxly conceived—came a conviction that fascism was the enemy of the working man and needed to be defeated at all costs. Spurred by that conviction, and perhaps in part by the feeling he later articulated of having "missed out" on the First World War, Orwell left England for Spain as soon as the manuscript of *Road to Wigan Pier* was completed, with the aim of aiding the democratically elected government of the Spanish Republic in their war against General Francisco Franco's insurgency.

The Spanish Civil War had broken out on July 17, 1936, when a junta of military generals staged a coup d'état against the government, a Popular Front coalition of centrist and left-wing parties. Franco soon emerged as the leader of the insurgency, which was driven to overthrow the government in reaction to its land reform programs and its strong anti-clericalism in a country where wealth and power had long been concentrated in the hands of a small Catholic elite. The leaders of the junta were not themselves fascists, but the coup drew the support of fascist elements within Spanish society as well as foreign fascist states. Mussolini's Italy supplied crucial material support to Franco's forces, including many of the airplanes used in the deadly campaigns against towns such as Guernica, whose bombardment was immortalized in Pablo Picasso's eponymous mural exhibited at the 1937 Paris International Exposition to raise funds to support the Republican government. As with the current conflict in Ukraine, the Republican government sought to garner support from the US and European democracies by presenting the conflict as a fight to defend democracy against tyranny. However, the Spanish prime minister was less effective than Volodymyr Zelenskyy; the US, Britain, and France maintained a strict policy of nonintervention in the conflict. As a result, the Republic became increasingly dependent on the Soviet Union, the only major power willing to supply it with weapons and other support.

To Orwell, as to many on the center and left of the political spectrum across the globe, including those African Americans who volunteered to fight in the Abraham Lincoln Battalion, the Western policy of nonintervention was unconscionable. Fighting alongside the Spanish Republican government against an insurgency backed by Mussolini and Hitler was an opportunity to deal a blow to fascism. It is a sign of his commitment to the anti-fascist struggle that, in leaving for Spain in December 1936, Orwell left behind his new wife, Eileen O'Shaughnessy Blair, whom he had married that June, only a year after the couple met at a party in his flat in London. Eileen was an intelligent and vivacious Oxford graduate who nonetheless devoted her short life (she died from complications from anesthesia during a minor operation in 1945, at age thirty-nine) to working as her husband's helpmeet, typing and occasionally editing his work, and enduring his occasional infidelities. She would eventually join Orwell in Spain, where she, too, risked her life on behalf of the Republican cause, although she receives only passing reference in his memoir of his time there, *Homage to Catalonia*, tellingly identified only as "my wife."

THE SPANISH CIVIL WAR WAS A CRUCIAL TURNING POINT IN Orwell's life. Had he died on the Spanish front—as he almost did, since a bullet through his throat came perilously close to doing more serious damage—it is unlikely that many today would remember his name. While *Road to Wigan Pier* was a masterful work of social investigation, it was not the stuff of enduring reputations. We remember Orwell because he wrote *Animal Farm* and *Nineteen Eighty-Four*, and he wrote those two books because of his experience in Spain.

Orwell arrived in Barcelona just just before the end of the year and, through a series of largely chance developments, enlisted in a regiment controlled by the Partido Obrero de Unificación Marxista (the Workers' Party of Marxist Unification), or POUM. The POUM were socialist revolutionaries who saw the war with Franco as an opportunity to radically reshape Spain, abolishing the vast inequalities of wealth and the resultant social and class divisions that beset Spanish society. Orwell considered the POUM to be terrible soldiers, but he developed an immense respect for their vision of egalitarian socialism, a vision that came to define his own socialist politics for the rest of his life. In June 1937, the Stalin-backed government initiated a witch hunt against the POUM and the similarly revolutionary-minded Anarchist party in Catalonia, whose revolutionary activity was perceived to be distracting from the war effort. Orwell sided with his comrades and developed what would be an enduring revulsion for the methods of Stalinist authoritarianism—including not only the torture and imprisonment of political opponents, but also, crucially, the manufacture of political disinformation to manipulate public opinion on the conflict.

He had gone to Spain determined to fight fascism. He left determined to expose the threat to liberty posed by Stalinism. *Homage to Catalonia* included a frank description of what he had seen of the conflict between the POUM and the Stalin-backed government in Barcelona. At the end of the book, Orwell explicitly states that he still supported the government against Franco's insurgents—"the war was worth winning even if the revolution was lost"—but the focus of much of the book is on the evils of Stalinism, with little discussion of Franco's politics.

———

HAD SPAIN NOT AWAKENED ORWELL TO THE DANGERS OF STALINism's totalitarian approach to political dissent, he would never have gone on to write *Animal Farm* or *Nineteen Eighty-Four*, the two books that have cemented his historical reputation as a champion of individual liberty against government tyranny.

Some have contended that *Animal Farm* and *Nineteen Eighty-Four* can be read as sequels of *Burmese Days*, critiques of the authoritarianism of the British Empire that Orwell so reviled. In a sense, this is true. Yet, while their enduring impact owes much to their ability to identify core truths about authoritarian regimes beyond Stalinist Russia, *Animal Farm* in particular is explicitly an allegory of the Russian Revolution, while *Nineteen Eighty-Four* is a dystopian fantasy set in the context of a Cold War between rival superpowers, one of which—Eurasia—is clearly modeled on the Soviet empire. (Orwell, notably, is recorded as the first person to have used the term *Cold War* in its modern context, in an October 1945 essay for *Tribune* entitled "You and the Atom Bomb.")

Both *Animal Farm* and *Nineteen Eighty-Four*, but especially the latter, are the culmination of an intellectual transformation more than two decades in the making. The Eric Blair who finished Eton in 1921 was a naive young snob, with little knowledge of the world beyond the confines of the British middle class.

His experiences in Burma, in Paris's Latin Quarter, among England's destitute in London and Wigan, and particularly in Catalonia developed his social conscience and honed his commitment to the twin ideals of liberty and social justice with which he remains indelibly associated.

2

THE THOUGHT POLICE

Censorship, Cancel Culture, and "Fake News"

Emblazoned behind an eight-foot-tall statue of George Orwell at the BBC headquarters at Broadcasting House in London is a line from an unpublished preface that Orwell wrote in 1945 to precede his novel *Animal Farm*: "If liberty means anything at all, it means the right to tell people what they do not want to hear." In erecting Orwell's statue in 2017, the BBC was honoring a disgruntled former employee who had gone on to become an international journalistic icon whose nonfiction writing is lionized for its clarity, integrity, and honesty. Viewed through that lens, the quote is a fitting tribute to Orwell's dedication to journalistic values.

In addition to telling hard truths, Orwell wrote in *Nineteen Eighty-Four* that the essence of liberty "is the freedom to say that two plus two make four. If that is granted, all else follows." Orwell's admirers have cited the quote as evidence both of his commitment to speaking the truth and of his commitment to free

speech. These two ideals were, however, frequently in tension in
Orwell's time, and nowhere is a similar tension between truth and
liberty clearer than in recent debates over political censorship and
cancel culture.

———

ORWELL OPPOSED CENSORSHIP—NOT ONLY OFFICIAL STATE CEN-
sorship, which was "obviously . . . not desirable," but also the pro-
cesses of informal censorship at work in societies that allegedly
embraced free speech, like Britain and its then empire. In *Burmese
Days*, he argued that the life of the Anglo-Indian was one in which
"every word and every thought is censored," not through formal
proscription but through the immense social pressure to fall in
line with the other members of the Anglo-Indian social elite. For
white Britons, India was a country where "there is no freedom of
speech, and merely to be overheard making a seditious remark
may damage [a man's] career."

Compared to Britain, India was a tyranny, yet Orwell did
not pretend that the "freeborn Englishman" living at home was
unconstrained by the forces of informal censorship that bound
his compatriots in the outposts of empire. The conviction that
certain things were "forbidden" to say out loud could be as true
in Britain as it was in India. As he wrote in an unpublished 1945
essay, "The Freedom of the Press," "If publishers and editors exert
themselves to keep certain topics out of print, it is not because they
are frightened of prosecution but because they are frightened of
public opinion. In this country intellectual cowardice is the worst
enemy a writer or journalist has to face."

Orwell first felt the sting of this informal censorship in 1937,
when his publisher, Victor Gollancz, refused to print *Homage to*

Catalonia, despite a prior understanding that Orwell would write a narrative of his time in Spain for the press. As mentioned in the previous chapter, before his arrival in Spain, Orwell's understanding of Spanish politics was limited to a belief that Franco was a fascist seeking to overthrow the democratically elected Republican government. While there, he realized that the situation was more complicated, and that the Soviet-backed government was committing atrocities against its own supporters, including many of Orwell's comrades in the revolutionary POUM militia, in the name of defending democracy. In Orwell's reckoning, "the real struggle in Spain, on the Government side, has been between revolution and counter-revolution; . . . the Government, though anxious enough to avoid being beaten by Franco, has been even more anxious to undo the revolutionary changes with which the outbreak of war was accompanied."

By the summer of 1937, the government's persecution of anyone associated with the POUM meant that Orwell risked arrest and imprisonment, and he and his wife, Eileen, fled the country in late June. Once back in England, he quickly wrote an unvarnished memoir of his experience, which included a discussion of the infighting within the Republican coalition, and sent it off to Gollancz, only for the publisher to reject his manuscript. For Gollancz, the issue was not that Orwell's analysis of the dynamics on the ground was incorrect as much as it was that it cast a gray shadow over the black-and-white argument in favor of supporting the Spanish government's battle against Franco. The Popular Front's argument was that the Republic was good and Franco was bad. They did not want to get into the gradation that the Republic was flawed, but that Franco was even worse.

Gollancz's refusal to publish *Homage to Catalonia* significantly muted Orwell's message among the British left. Gollancz was the publisher of the Left Book Club series. Orwell's *The Road to Wigan Pier* had been published in the LBC series in 1936, and the book represented his first commercial success. In 1939, LBC membership exceeded fifty thousand people who were a key pillar of the Popular Front coalition in Britain, an alliance of Labour supporters, Liberals, Communists, and unaffiliated progressives opposed to fascism, and were broadly supportive of the Soviet Union. While many of the LBC members identified as pacifists, the club's politics were supportive of the Republican cause in the Spanish Civil War, and the LBC organized fundraisers in support of the Spanish Republic.

Although Orwell was ultimately able to find a small publisher to put out *Homage to Catalonia*, the book initially sold only a few hundred copies and was not widely read by socialists in Britain. The revolutionary left in Britain, those who could be expected to sympathize with the ambitions of the Trotskyists and anarchists among whom Orwell served in Spain, and whom he saw persecuted, imprisoned, and executed by the Republican government, were deeply invested in the war against Franco, and naturally suspicious of any reports threatening to discredit Franco's opponents. Without the backing of the LBC, Orwell had little hope of his reports being taken seriously by his intended audience.

Yet, Orwell was not entirely unsympathetic to Gollancz's position. As he wrote to another editor in February 1938, "I do not agree with this view, because I hold the outmoded opinion that in the long run it does not pay to tell lies, but in so far as it was dictated by a desire to help the Spanish Government, I can respect it." Years later, he put a name to the reason for the informal silencing he experienced: "It is a sort of charm or incantation to silence uncomfortable truths. When you are told that by saying this, that or the other you are 'playing into the hands of some sinister enemy,' you know that it is your duty to shut up immediately." But, even if Orwell could understand the logic behind refraining from playing into the hands of the enemy, it was a duty that he was unwilling to accept. Several years later, he would run into similar opposition from publishers who had been briefed by the government not to take on his novel *Animal Farm*, given its potential to anger the Soviet leadership at a time when the United Kingdom was allied with the Soviet Union in the war against Hitler.

———

BOTH *HOMAGE TO CATALONIA* AND *ANIMAL FARM* WERE, OF course, ultimately published, and the latter book achieved a massive circulation in both the UK and the US even before the Cold War began to heat up. The refusal of private publishers to take on Orwell's work may have vexed and inconvenienced him, but it is not akin to the full-throttled state censorship he depicts in either *Animal Farm* or *Nineteen Eighty-Four*. Today, several self-professed victims of cancel culture, from both the left and the right of the political spectrum, have repeatedly denounced attempts to de-platform them as "Orwellian." In reality, these episodes of corporate "cancellation" are more akin to the politically motivated boycotts of Orwell's work by publishers than to the totalitarian exercise of state power by the Ingsoc (short for "English socialism") regime in *Nineteen Eighty-Four*.

When Twitter (now known as X) banned his father from the social media platform in the aftermath of the January 6, 2021, uprising at the US Capitol, Donald Trump Jr. responded with a tweet of his own: "We are living Orwell's 1984. Free-speech no longer exists in America. It died with big tech and what's left is only there for a chosen few." That same day, Missouri senator—and proponent of Trump's false claims to have won the 2020 election—Josh Hawley offered a raised fist to those assembled outside the Capitol just hours before the mob turned violent. In response to the news that the publisher Simon & Schuster had decided to cancel his book contract as a consequence of his defense of the insurrectionists, he, too, posted a tweet: "This could not be more Orwellian. Only approved speech can now be published. This is the Left looking to cancel everyone they don't approve of. I will fight this cancel culture with everything I have." In reality, of course, neither Trump nor Hawley were silenced after Janaury 2021. Trump continued to broadcast his election conspiracies on his alternative media platform Truth Social, and Hawley's book came out with Regnery Publishing later that year.

Nonetheless, references to "Orwellian" practices within the supposedly liberal media continued with a vengeance two years later when Tesla CEO Elon Musk launched his war on Twitter, ultimately buying the company in October 2022, purging its leadership, and reinstating the accounts of several right-wing figures who had been banned from the site. Musk had repeatedly criticized Twitter for its deplatforming of right-wing extremists, warning in Orwellian tones, "This is a battle for the future of civilization. If free speech is lost even in America, tyranny is all that lies ahead." Within weeks of taking control of the media platform, he reinstated Donald Trump's account, although the former president decided that he preferred to continue to use Truth Social to broadcast his views. (Trump ultimately returned to the platform in August 2023, posting a defiant picture of his Fulton County, Georgia, mug shot.) Musk also began to selectively release internal company documents to a group of right-wing journalists, in what became known as the "Twitter Files." Among the political right, the material within these files was proof of an "Orwellian conspiracy" of "shadow banning" by the company. "Shadow banning," or "visibility filtering," was the alleged practice by Twitter of secretly suppressing exposure of certain tweets on the platform. The Fox News headline "Tech guru slams Twitter shadow banning as 'one step away from George Orwell's Thought Police'" was typical of the conservative media's coverage of Musk's "Twitter Files" leaks. When members of the government questioned whether Twitter under Musk might become a platform for extremist disinformation, the *New York Post* editorial team sprang to his defense:

> Even the White House is getting in on the action, with chief flack Karine Jean-Pierre hint-threatening Monday, "We're all keeping a close eye on" Twitter under Musk. To do what exactly? Is the government going to try to force Twitter to silence people?
>
> Pure Orwell. But Musk (so far) seems unfazed. And that's great for Twitter, journalism and America in general.

Ironically, within weeks of the *Post*'s editorial, the media world was aflame with reports that Musk had suddenly evicted several high-profile journalists from Twitter, with the result that now it was the left accusing those on their right of being Orwellian. Gil Duran, one of the deplatformed journalists, wrote in the *San Francisco Chronicle*:

> News outlets in particular must resist this outrageous attack on press freedom and start planning an orderly transition away from Musk's Twitter. . . .

In George Orwell's "1984," the main character spends his days at the Ministry of Truth, revising history to suit the dictatorship's specifications. This involves deleting the existence of "unpersons"—people whose existence has been erased on orders from on high.

When Twitter disabled my account, I briefly felt the sensation of being an "unperson." Then again, Twitter is not real life. I'm probably better off without it.

Duran is a comparatively moderate member of the political left, having previously worked as a speechwriter for former California governor Jerry Brown. On the far left of the political spectrum, meanwhile, supporters of former British Labour Party leader Jeremy Corbyn have deployed similar rhetoric against what they perceive to be efforts to cancel Corbyn's supporters within the party. The blog *Labour Heartlands* wrote in July 2020 that the party's investigations into alleged antisemitism among Corbyn supporters amounted to little more than "Orwellian Grass/Cancel Culture which has shut down free speech and debate," a seeming reference to members of the Labour Party "grassing" (informing) on their colleagues for using unacceptable antisemitic language. The blog went on to assert that, by calling out allegedly antisemitic language, Labour's central office was fostering an Orwellian "environment of 'Newspeak,' a culture of fear and guarded expression of opinion." In a particularly ironic twist, the *Labour Heartlands* blog compared the left's perceived persecution by the Labour Party on allegedly overblown charges of antisemitism to *Nineteen Eighty-Four*'s ritualized "two minutes hate" in which the regime "allow[s] the citizens of Oceania to vent their existential anguish and personal hatreds toward politically expedient enemies . . . specifically Emmanuel Goldstein and his followers." The scapegoating of Goldstein in *Nineteen Eighty-Four* is a clear and intentional reference to, and condemnation of, antisemitism within both the Nazi and Stalinist regimes.

Hawley and Trump Jr. on the right, Duran from the center, and *Labour Heartlands* on the left all believed that Orwell would have been on their side, defending their right to free speech against the Thought Police's attempts to cancel them. But would he?

That question gets to the tension that we identified at the opening of the chapter between Orwell's commitment to free speech and his commitment to the truth. Perhaps the best, if slightly circuitous, route to answering that question comes via an exploration of what many perceive to be the most controversial aspect of Orwell's legacy: his decision to prepare a list in 1949 of "unreliable" political authors for the British government—a list that effectively guaranteed that those authors would be blackballed from government employment.

GOLLANCZ WAS NOT THE ONLY PUBLISHER TO CENSOR ORWELL'S views on the Spanish Civil War. Orwell also found his views silenced by another key figure of the literary Popular Front, Kingsley Martin, the long-serving editor of the *New Statesman*. At the same time that he sent his manuscript to Gollancz, Orwell sent Martin an article about his experience, "Eyewitness in Spain," which the latter refused to publish. Martin attempted to assuage Orwell's resentment by sending him a copy of Franz Borkenau's *The Spanish Cockpit* to review, but when Orwell submitted his essay to the *New Statesman*'s editors, Martin wrote to Orwell in July 1937 that "it is not possible for us to use your review of *The Spanish Cockpit*.

The reason is simply that it too far controverts the political policy of the paper. It is very uncompromisingly said and implies that our Spanish correspondents are all wrong."

In his review, Orwell had written, "The most important fact that has emerged from the whole business is that the Communist Party is now (presumably for the sake of Russian Foreign Policy) an anti-revolutionary force." Orwell went on to say of his own experience in Spain that "the atmosphere in Barcelona, what with the ceaseless arrests [of POUM members and anarchists accused of undermining the Republic], the censored newspapers and the prowling hordes of police, was like a nightmare." It was a nightmare he vividly portrayed in the final chapters of *Homage to Catalonia*, and from which he drew in crafting the dystopian landscape of *Nineteen Eighty-Four*. Orwell's official biographer, Bernard Crick, had no more sympathy than Orwell for Martin's decision, writing that the editor "never seemed to grasp the enormity of his action, particularly reprehensible as he never denied that Orwell's facts were true, only that he believed that to publish them would damage the Popular Front. . . . Orwell thought that such 'expediency' was toleration of 'necessary murder' and showed 'the mentality of the whore'—a willingness to string along at any price." While Orwell continued to write for the *New Statesman*, he never forgave Martin. Shortly before his death, Orwell exacted his revenge on Martin by including him on the list he gave the British government of authors he perceived to be dangerously sympathetic to the Soviet Union.

———

"THE LIST," AS IT BECAME KNOWN, WAS COMPILED FOR THE INFORMATION Research Department, a branch of the British Foreign

Office, at the behest of Orwell's close friend Celia Kirwan, who then worked for the IRD, while Orwell was in the hospital in the spring of 1949. (Kirwan was one of the many women to whom he unsuccessfully proposed marriage after Eileen's death, but the two still remained on close terms.) The IRD was formed by Clement Attlee's Labour government in 1948, in the early days of the Cold War, with the aim of combating pro-Soviet propaganda, in part by dispelling Soviet disinformation and in part by generating its own disinformation campaigns against the Soviet Union, the latter brief being clandestine and classified activity of which Orwell may well not have been aware. In soliciting the list of names from Orwell, Kirwan was seeking to identify authors with whom the IRD should not work because they lacked anti-communist *bona fides*. The list was culled from notes that Orwell had compiled over the years about "crypto-communists and fellow travellers." He had never shied away from denouncing colleagues by name for their subservience to the Stalinist line. His frequently misunderstood 1940 essay "Inside the Whale" is in large part a criticism of the hollow and false writing produced by pro-Soviet intellectuals in the 1930s, and not, as some have perceived it, an endorsement of political quietism or disengagement. Kirwan rightly guessed that he would have few qualms about repeating his denunciations to the government.

The list itself was not released by the British state archives until 2003. However, by that time, the notebooks from which Orwell's comments had been culled had been known about for years. Thus, in 2002, Christopher Hitchens was able to surmise that Kingsley Martin was on the list, as he is marked down in Orwell's notebooks as "Decayed liberal. Very dishonest." (The actual notes that Orwell provided to the IRD on Martin are even more damning:

"?? Too dishonest to be outright 'crypto' or fellow-traveller, but reliably pro-Russian on all major issues.")

For many on the left, Orwell's decision to provide the Attlee government with the list was a betrayal. Timothy Garton Ash, who first published a copy of the full list in the *Guardian* in June 2003, noted that its existence had led to the publication of many articles with lurid headlines such as "Big Brother of the Foreign Office," "Socialist Icon Who Became an Informer," and "How Orwell's Blacklist Aided Secret Service," causing Orwell's reputation among the left to suffer "a body-blow from which it may never recover," as James Oliver and Paul Lashmar wrote in *Britain's Secret Propaganda War*.

On one level, this was obviously untrue, as most readers of *Animal Farm* or *Nineteen Eighty-Four* remain completely unaware of Orwell's collaboration with the IRD. But for Orwell fans and those on the activist left, particularly in Britain, the disclosures had a serious impact on his reputation. Oliver went on to say, "To some, it was as if Winston Smith had willingly cooperated with the Thought Police in *Nineteen Eighty-Four*." This was definitely the attitude of one of my former students, a passionate young self-identified Trotskyist, who came into my classroom knowing little more about Orwell than that he had, in her understanding, betrayed his comrades on the left by publishing "The List."

Orwell's supporters, including the late Christopher Hitchens, have sought to defend him by arguing that his list was not intended to land anyone in prison, but merely to ensure that they did not receive publishing commissions from the government. As Celia Kirwan said to Ash shortly before her death, "The only thing that was going to happen to them was that they wouldn't be asked to write for the Information Research Department." In the end, this turned out to be true, but Orwell could not have known it at the time. Not long before he gave his list to the British government, the Hollywood studios had publicly blacklisted a group of screenwriters and directors who became known as the "Hollywood Ten" after they had been branded as communist sympathizers by the US House Un-American Activities Committee (HUAC). The hysteria and overreaction that ensued led to the blacklisting of hundreds of artists and intellectuals, many on the most spurious of pretenses. With the perspective of hindsight, the HUAC witch hunts are almost impossible to justify. Yet, it is notable that, at the time, William Phillips and Philip Rahv, the editors of the New York–based *Partisan Review*, for which Orwell wrote regularly until his death, believed that the authors condemned by the committee were only reaping what they had sown by acting as propagandists for the Soviet Union.

Orwell's willingness to take part in a similar exercise in Britain reflects the same conviction and reveals his privileging of truth over freedom of speech when the two came into direct conflict. While Orwell abhorred censorship, he was willing to do his part to ensure that authors whom he perceived to be knowingly mendacious were not offered a platform to voice their untruths, because truthfulness was, in Orwell's estimation, the highest virtue. His journalistic writing is peppered with phrases such as "This was true enough," "The truth was that," "It would be true to say," and "I believe this was true."

In February 1944, Orwell published a column on the nature of truth. He began with the example of the Nazis airing fictitious radio reports of bombing raids over Britain:

> Now, we are aware that those raids did not happen. But what
> use would our knowledge be if the Germans conquered

Britain? For the purposes of a future historian, did those raids happen, or didn't they? The answer is: If Hitler survives, they happened, and if he falls, they didn't happen. So with innumerable other events of the past ten or twenty years. . . . Did Trotsky plot with the Nazis? How many German aeroplanes were shot down in the Battle of Britain? Does Europe welcome the New Order? In no case do you get one answer which is universally accepted because it is true: in each case you get a number of totally incompatible answers, one of which is finally adopted as the result of a physical struggle. History is written by the winners.

Read in one light, the passage suggests a postmodernist approach to reality as merely a discursive construct. As Donald Trump's former advisor Kellyanne Conway famously posited in 2017: there were facts, and then there were "alternative facts." But for all his instinctive libertarianism, Orwell could never endorse a world in which "alternative facts" were given free rein. Characteristically, he concluded the above-quoted essay with a backhanded compliment to his own country. Objective truths mattered, and, "In the last analysis our [Britain's] only claim to victory is that, if we win the war, we shall tell fewer lies about it than our adversaries."

Orwell's commitment to objective truth explains why he describes the essence of freedom in *Nineteen Eighty-Four* as the right to say that $2 + 2 = 4$, not the right to say that $2 + 2 = 5$. As I noted in the introduction, it is dangerous to ascribe opinions to someone long dead. Yet, here the weight and consistency of the evidence is overwhelming. In a free society, citizens should theoretically be able to proclaim $2 + 2$ to be whatever they want it to be. But that is not Orwell's idea of freedom from censorship. Orwell believed in liberty above all else, but liberty, in his view, was predicated on an assumption of personal and social responsibility.

So, to return to our earlier question, what would Orwell have had to say to modern political extremists such as Josh Hawley, who cloak themselves in Orwellian outrage at the censorship of their proclamations that $2 + 2 = 5$? While he probably would not have viewed it expedient or worthwhile to actively censor extremist voices, Orwell certainly would not have claimed those extremists as allies and would not have endorsed publishers such as Simon & Schuster or social media outlets like Twitter giving them a platform.

The weight of evidence suggests that Orwell would have been more disturbed by the mendacity of those claiming to have been canceled than he would have been by the decision of some media not to publish them. For one thing, he would have recognized that, in a pluralistic democracy like the United States or the United Kingdom, being deplatformed by a private media outlet is not the same as being censored by an authoritarian state. Just as Orwell ultimately published both *Homage to Catalonia* and *Animal Farm* with Secker & Warburg, in contemporary Western democracies, individuals who are "canceled" by X (formerly Twitter) can find an alternative platform on Truth Social, Threads, or any number of alternative sites, and while alleged antisemites may be thrown out of the Labour Party, they are not vaporized, nor are they rendered unpersons and deleted from the historical record as happens in *Nineteen Eighty-Four*'s Oceania. Josh Hawley is still a US senator. Jeremy Corbyn is still an MP. They can, and do, still make their voices heard. While Orwell did not agree with Gollancz's decision not to publish *Homage*, nor with the poet and publisher T. S. Eliot's decision not to take on *Animal Farm* for Faber & Faber, he accepted that, in a democratic society, they were within their rights not to publish his work. He even continued to collaborate with Gollancz after he rejected *Homage*. He never pretended that the politically motivated blackballing that he faced was akin to the fate suffered by Winston Smith at the hands of the Thought Police.

———

HAD ORWELL LIVED SEVENTY-FIVE YEARS LATER, HE MIGHT HAVE used the word *gaslighting* to describe his experience of having publishers and colleagues on the left repeatedly attempt to convince him that the horrors he had seen officials of the Republican government perpetuate against their supposed allies in Spain were insignificant in the context of the fight against Franco. The term traces its origins to Orwell's era. It references the 1938 play *Gas Light* by the British playwright Patrick Hamilton, later remade into not one, but two films in Orwell's lifetime—first, in 1940, a British production, starring Anton Walbrook and Diana Wynyard, and then, in 1944, a Hollywood remake, directed by George Cukor and starring Ingrid Bergman and Charles Boyer. It is likely that Orwell saw at least one of these productions, given the ubiquity of cinema attendance in the 1940s. The central conceit of the play and the films is that the husband wants to drive his wife to a breakdown by convincing her that she is crazy in order to get his hands on extraordinary jewels. One way he does this is to deny that the gaslights in their home are dimming, even though he orchestrates that action. When the term first entered general parlance in the 1960s, it was used to reference an abusive relationship in which a person manipulates their victim and causes them to question the validity of their own thoughts and their perception of reality. This is arguably what Gollancz and Martin sought to do to Orwell. He came back from Spain convinced that the Republican government's suppression of its own allies was an atrocity that merited publicity, and the two editors tried unsuccessfully to convince him that it was an insignificant misfortune in the context of the larger truth of the civil war.

So, he might well have argued that he was being gaslit under the pretext of not wanting to play into the hands of enemy. At the same time, he might not, as he hated few linguistic tropes more than what he termed "dying metaphors"—hackneyed phrases that had "been twisted out of their original meaning without those who use them even being aware of the fact." Orwell, ever the great list maker, identified the following as dying metaphors: "ring the changes on," "take up the cudgels for," "toe the line," "ride roughshod over," "stand shoulder to shoulder with," "play into the hands of," "no axe to grind," "grist to the mill," "fishing in troubled waters," "on the order of the day," "Achilles' heel," "swan song," and "hotbed." The term *gaslighting* has become so ubiquitous of late that it has arguably become a phrase worthy of inclusion in his list.

In November of 2022, dictionary publisher Merriam-Webster declared *gaslighting* its word of the year, citing a 1,740 percent increase in lookups of the word by online dictionary users. During the #MeToo movement starting in the late 2010s, gaslighting evolved from its original meaning of pscyhological manipulation and came to refer specifically to the manipulation of a woman by a male perpetrator in order to exercise his power over her. However, by the time that Merriam-Webster declared it the word of the year, gaslighting had lost both its gendered connotation and its contextual specificity. As the dictionary announced, "in recent years, we have seen the meaning of gaslighting refer also to something simpler and broader: 'the act or practice of grossly misleading someone, especially for a personal advantage.' In this use, the word is at home with other terms relating to modern forms of deception and manipulation, such as *fake news*, *deepfake*, and *artificial intelligence*." *Orwellian* is another term frequently grouped in this company.

Whether Orwell would have embraced the term *gaslighting* as an apt analogy for the manipulation of truth by those with power or viewed it as a dead metaphor remains unanswerable. Perhaps he would have appreciated the term if it had cleaved more closely to its original meaning, as a form of psychological manipulation. In *Nineteen Eighty-Four*, O'Brien, one of the Thought Police and the architect of Winston and Julia's torture, strove to gaslight them through the torture he meted out in Room 101 in the basement of the Ministry of Truth. Before the Party would take Winston and Julia's lives (which it promised him it ultimately would do), it set about taking their minds. Before their arrest, the two are convinced that, while they will inevitably be tortured and forced to confess to all sorts of crimes, their inner thoughts and feelings will remain their own. As Julia says, "They can make you say anything—anything—but they can't make you believe it. They can't get inside you." Yet, that is exactly what the Party does. It breaks Winston's hold on reality, leaving him unsure of whether anything he once believed is true, even the existence of the law of gravity. As O'Brien, his interrogator, tells Winston, "Reality is inside the skull," and once he has broken his mind, he will be able to control his reality, such that, if he chose, he could turn invisible or "float off this floor like a soap bubble" in front of Winston's eyes.

ANY DISCUSSION OF ORWELL'S CONTRIBUTION TO DEBATES AROUND the politics of language cannot limit itself to his views on censorship and free speech, or truth and falsehood, crucial as these issues were both to Orwell's political age and to our own. He was equally outspoken about the ways in which dishonest politics unconsciously but inevitably corrupts political discourse and language more broadly. Orwell denounced the deliberate propagation of what we would now term disinformation, but he was, for much of his life, a self-conscious propagandist, in the sense of promoting a political position through his writings. Writing in 1946, he claimed that the bulk of his published work had been motivated by "political purpose," by the "[d]esire to push the world in a certain direction, to alter other people's idea of the kind of society that they should strive after."

Two of my favorite Orwell essays deal with the craft of political writing, both in its intention and its execution. In each, he acknowledges and dissects the tension between political writing and art. Lies and censorship were not the only means of silencing and distorting truth. Political writing, even when not outright mendacious, is often intended to misdirect and mislead, and, as a consequence, Orwell argues, is often bad writing.

The first of these two essays, "Politics and the English Language," published in *Horizon* magazine in April 1946, is an intentionally tendentious work, aimed at highlighting the connection between bad political thought and bad political writing. The essay includes one of the many Orwell lines that never fails to make me laugh out loud, when he notes that, in bad political writing, "the passive voice is wherever possible used in preference to the active."

(I once listened to a podcast in which three lexicographers tore Orwell apart for using the passive voice in that sentence, and I thought, *Can't you see the joke?*)

Orwell suggests that it is possible to avoid the trap of writing and speaking bad English by self-consciously avoiding "bad habits which spread by imitation," including the use, not only of passive voice, but also of so-called "dead metaphors," euphemism, and grandiose words from Latin roots. "If one gets rid of these habits one can think more clearly, and to think clearly is a necessary first step toward political regeneration." Here, he seems to be saying that if readers and writers are conscious of language, they will cease to be susceptible to corrupt political argument. Totalitarianism will lose its strength in the face of crisp, clear prose. It is a heavy burden to place on the shoulders of the English language. That Orwell was willing to assign language such power underscored his belief in the centrality of speech to politics, and the importance not only of securing free speech, but of ensuring that words that are spoken freely are also spoken honestly.

Orwell's second piece about the power of language is "Why I Write," a brief essay that he published shortly after "Politics and the English Language." In "Why I Write," Orwell attempts to set himself apart from the crowd by making the claim that he, at least, had always attempted to reconcile the aesthetic and the political in his own writing:

> What I have most wanted to do throughout the past ten years is to make political writing into an art. My starting point is always a feeling of partisanship, a sense of injustice. When I sit down to write a book, I do not say to myself, "I am going to produce a work of art." I write it because there

is some lie that I want to expose, some fact to which I want
to draw attention, and my initial concern is to get a hearing.
But I could not do the work of writing a book, or even a long
magazine article, if it were not also an aesthetic experience.

The two essays offer an important window into how Orwell
perceived the link between politics and language, beyond his
focus on censorship and outright lying. He believed that political
writing could be crisp and aesthetic, and he strove to ensure that
his own work met those standards; but political writing could only
read clearly and beautifully if the ideologies and acts it propagated
were equally pure. Anti-totalitarianism and genuine, communitarian socialism, in Orwell's view, fit this description. Stalinism
and imperialism—be it Nazi imperialism, British imperialism,
or the new global hegemony exercised by the United States—
did not. When politics consists of "the defence of the indefensible . . . political language has to consist largely of euphemism,
question-begging and sheer cloudy vagueness." Orwell—ever
the lover of lists— makes this generalization concrete with three
apposite examples from his own political moment, which continue to resonate in ours:

Defenceless villages are bombarded from the air, the inhabitants driven out into the countryside, the cattle machine-
gunned, the huts set on fire with incendiary bullets: this is
called *pacification*. Millions of peasants are robbed of their
farms and sent trudging along the roads with no more than
they can carry: this is called *transfer of population* or *rectifi-
cation of frontiers*. People are imprisoned for years without
trial, or shot in the back of the neck or sent to die of scurvy

in Arctic lumber camps: this is called *elimination of unreliable elements.*

Politicians and propagandists of all sorts resort to ungainly
euphemisms, he argues, when they feel unable to communicate
their message honestly for fear that the listener will recoil. Thus,
a fellow-traveling member of the British left cannot defend the
Stalinist purges by stating it is okay to murder your political enemies. Instead, Orwell gives a parody of a typical fellow-traveling
linguistic contortion:

> While freely conceding that the Soviet regime exhibits
> certain features which the humanitarian may be inclined
> to deplore, we must, I think, agree that a certain curtail-
> ment of the right to political opposition is an unavoid-
> able concomitant of transitional periods, and that the
> rigors which the Russian people have been called upon to
> undergo have been amply justified in the sphere of con-
> crete achievement.

Such obfuscation, Orwell argues, helps to reconcile the listener to
the indefensible arguments put forth by the speaker, thus creating a toxic spiral in which the listener may become a propagator
of similar linguistic and factual distortions. It's a vicious circle, as
when a man "take[s] to drink because he feels himself to be a failure, and then fail[s] all the more completely because he drinks."

———

ORWELL EXPANDS UPON THIS LINK BETWEEN SPEECH AND
thought in "The Principles of Newspeak," an appendix to *Nine-*

teen Eighty-Four that lays out how the bureaucratic language of Oceania functions. "The Principles of Newspeak" outlines a system of language consciously premised on obfuscation. The Newspeak "B vocabulary" covered political language. "No word in the B vocabulary was ideologically neutral. A great many were euphemisms. Such words, for instance, as *joycamp* (forced-labour camp) or *Minipax* (Ministry of Peace, i.e. Ministry of War) meant almost the exact opposite of what they appeared to mean."

It is easy to think of examples of this kind of speech in our own political discourse, as when the UK government's Regulatory Policy Committee produced a brief indicating that the controversial policy of benefit rationalization known as Universal Credit would "ensure that appropriate conditions of entitlement are applied to claimants," rather than saying it would potentially reduce benefit levels for many vulnerable recipients. Another example would be the language used in the debate over abortion rights. Critics of the term "pro-life" contend that it elides the reality that anti-abortion activists value the potential life of an unborn fetus higher than the life of the mother. Such loaded terms are not lies per se, but they are equally not honest truths. And, Orwell would argue, they do not make for good prose.

The appendix on Newspeak is written as a history cum manual of the "language," which, at the purported time of its writing had not yet superseded "Oldspeak," or Standard English, but which was rapidly gaining ground as both a written and spoken dialect. According to the manual, "The purpose of Newspeak was not only to provide a medium of expression for the world-view and mental habits proper to the devotees of [the Party], but to make all other modes of thought impossible." Orwell, as so often in his writing, makes the abstract theory concrete by use of an apposite example:

"The word *free* still existed in Newspeak, but it could only be used in such statements as 'This dog is free from lice' or 'This field is free from weeds.' . . . [P]olitical and intellectual freedom no longer existed even as concepts." The end goal of this streamlining of language was the abolition of history, "History had already been rewritten, but when Oldspeak had been once and for all superseded, the last link with the past would have been severed."

For me as a historian, Orwell's dystopian prophecy that, if certain language could be eliminated, the realities it had described would in effect cease to exist is one of the most frightening of *Nineteen Eighty-Four*'s many nightmares. Orwell argues that, without a language in which to express ideas such as liberty, oppression, or romantic love, those concepts would cease to have a meaning for us and effectively be extinguished from our consciousness.

It's a difficult idea to come to terms with. Is the existence of oppression really contingent on our ability to articulate it? Your instinctive answer might be: of course not. But that proposition seems less far-fetched when we consider it in the context of the battles over language taking place in classrooms, courtrooms, and government offices today.

We can clearly see the risks of "reality control" or "doublethink" in Russian president Vladimir Putin's efforts to reconstruct his country's invasion of Ukraine as a liberating "special operation." If you cannot say Russia invaded Ukraine, did it?

But Newspeak is not only on the rise outside the West. In the United States, we see attempts to control reality through the control of language in Florida's 2022 "Don't Say Gay" law, prohibiting the discussion of gender identity or sexual orientation in kindergarten through the third grade (and discouraging its discussion in middle and high school classrooms). The intent of this and similar legislation is to stamp out queer sexualities by prohibiting their discussion. A similar threat exists in Oklahoma's House Bill 1775, signed into law in May 2021, which, among other things, proscribes the teaching of any curriculum that might cause a student to "feel discomfort, guilt, anguish or any other form of psychological distress on account of his or her race or sex." More than a dozen other states have introduced similar legislation to outlaw discussion in classrooms of systemic racism or sexism. In addition to this proscriptive legislation, some states and districts have gone as far as to dictate what should be taught. Florida has once again shown itself a leader in this field, with Governor Ron DeSantis's endorsement of new board of education curriculum standards in July 2023 that mandate teaching that some slaves benefited from the experience of slavery.

These laws have had disruptive effects on classroom teaching, as when a Florida teacher was subjected to a disciplinary investigation in 2023 after showing the Disney film *Strange World* to her class of ten- and eleven-year-olds as part of a lesson on ecosystems and the environment. The teacher was focused on the plot of the film, which revolves around a family of explorers, but parents expressed concern that the film featured an openly gay character. But the disruption and uncertainty of this legislation for educators pales in the face of the laws' implicit intent. If it is illegal to identify systemic racism, let alone discuss its causes and possible remedies, it constrains the potential for, if not outright prohibits, social change. If young people cannot discuss the existence of queer identities, they may be left unable to recognize and make sense of thoughts and feelings they are experiencing in ways that would allow them to gain a consciousness of their own sexual or gender identity.

Linked to these laws prohibiting discussion is a rise in the banning of books in school libraries across the United States with the aim of curtailing thought and discussion of topics such as homosexuality, queer identities, and racism. In the state of Virginia, school boards in 2022 banned several dozen titles, including works by the Nobel laureate Toni Morrison dealing with race and sexuality, *Gender Queer: A Memoir* by Maia Kobabe, and *Good Trouble: Lessons from the Civil Rights Playbook* by Christopher Noxon. But Virginia is nowhere near the worst offender when it comes to banning books. According to an analysis by PEN America, Texas, Pennsylvania, Florida, Oklahoma, and Kansas ranked highest in terms of the number of titles banned in those states, with a whopping 713 books under some form of ban in the state of Texas in April 2022. Each of these represents an effort at controlling reality by controlling speech, an effort that Senator Chris Murphy of Connecticut correctly identified as "downright Orwellian."

THE ISSUE OF INTELLECTUAL SILENCING IS AS PERTINENT TO THE history of Britain as to that of the United States. For over a decade, Britain's schools and universities have found themselves in a pitched faceoff with members of successive Conservative governments and right-wing pundits in what has become known as the "History Wars." The politicization of the British history curriculum dates back to February 2013, when the then education minister Michael Gove proposed a new national curriculum that, in the words of Cambridge's Regius Professor of History Richard Evans, sought to "us[e] history teaching in our schools to impart a patriotic sense of national identity through the uncritical hero-worship of great men and women from the British past." The author and broadcaster Simon Schama was less diplomatic, noting that one of Gove's proposed heroes, Lord Clive, the eighteenth-century governor-general of India and hero of the Seven Years' War, was in reality a "sociopathic, corrupt thug," someone who made "our most dodgy bankers look like a combination of Mary Poppins and Jesus Christ."

The 2013 controversy centered around the blinkered narrowness of Gove's new curriculum, but in the years that followed, educators and Gove's successors have squared off over the extent to which teachers should or should not be required to teach the darker side of Britain's history in their classrooms. The Black Curriculum campaign gained momentum in tandem with the British Black Lives Matter movement, which in 2020 targeted visual symbols of historical whitewashing in the form of statues, including that of the seventeenth-century slave trader Edward Colston in Bristol, and the statue of the South African mining magnate and imperial adventurer Cecil Rhodes at Oriel College, Oxford. In Oxford, Ndjodi Ndeunyema, a PhD student involved in the Rhodes protests, articulated the link between the statues and the censoring of Black history: "That history [of Rhodes's imperialist atrocities] will never be erased, it's a lived reality for people in southern Africa, but it needs to be contextualised, it needs to be accurately represented and not glorified in the way it is today." The BLM movement has emphasized that, like the control and manipulation of language, the control and manipulation of the iconography of the public square is a crucial vehicle for suppressing and rewriting history. Debates over the public veneration of those guilty of racial atrocities have not been limited to Britain. The Oxford University activists were inspired by the Rhodes Must Fall campaign launched at the University of Cape Town in 2015 with the aim of removing a 1934 statue of the imperialist from its prominent position on the university campus. (The statue was ultimately taken down and put in storage.) In 2021, statues of Confederate general and Virginia native son Robert E. Lee were removed from plinths in Charlottesville and Richmond, with the latter statue moved to the city's Black History Museum. In France, activists have unsuccessfully called for the removal of a statue of Jean-Baptiste Colbert, finance minister to King Louis XIV, who drafted the "*code noir*," which regulated the treatment of slaves within the French colonies, from its plinth in front of the French parliament.

Debates over the campaigns around the public presentation of statues have repeatedly referenced Orwell, both in defense and in admonition of the protestors' campaigns. In June 2020, the conservative *New York Post* came out with an editorial denouncing statue toppling, likening the movement to events in Orwell's *Nineteen Eighty-Four* and citing this passage: "Every record has been destroyed or falsified, every book rewritten, every picture has been repainted, every statue and street building has been renamed, every date has been altered. And the process is continuing day by day and minute by minute. History has stopped." It continued by stating that the quotation was perfect for this moment, before going on to criticize the actions of BLM protestors, asserting, "These mobs aren't trying to effect change; they're flaunting their power," and calling on those in positions of power among the progressive left to denounce the movement. The editorial ended with a second allusion to Orwell: "The real lesson of history, though, is that appeasing the mob only inspires it to look for more to destroy. We're still a long way from '1984' but getting closer."

Two years later, an opinion piece in the *Jerusalem Post* quoted the same passage from *Nineteen Eighty-Four* in an effort to expose what the author perceived to be the historical distortions underpinning the alliance of Palestinian activists with the BLM movement. The article quoted even more extensively from Orwell's novel, highlighting Winston's observation to Julia that the citizens of Oceania "could be made to accept the most flagrant violations of reality, because they never fully grasped the enormity of what was demanded of them, and were not sufficiently interested in public events to notice what was happening." According to Ruthie Blum, a former senior editor at the *Jerusalem Post* and the author of the piece, the lies that the public is swallowing are not that the men represented by the statues were heroic figures, but that the Palestinian activists were anything other than "self-defined intersectional victims out to destroy the foundations of the very societies that grant them the freedom to do so." She went on to accuse "many liberals, among them Jews" of supporting a false "reality, in the pursuit of political correctness or to avoid, at all costs, accusations of racism." The conservative Black British commentator Calvin Robinson, known for frequent criticisms of BLM and the calls for a Black curriculum in British schools, wrote in the *Daily Mail* in 2020 that training against unconscious race bias was political correctness turned Orwellian and made an analogy to the Thought Police—who, he claimed, wanted "to control minds by delving into the unconscious, where they would like to eradicate unpalatable ideas and impose compliance."

In these readings, the anti-racist activists are the Thought Police intent on destroying history. Others, however, have pushed back against such interpretations, arguing that they fundamentally misrepresent the dynamics of power in modern Western society. Thus, the Cornell University–based historian of Europe, Enzo Traverso, in a widely reprinted article first published in *Jacobin* magazine in June 2020, argued, "These examples are misleading comparisons, because they refer to the erasure of the past by the powerful. Yet, anti-racist iconoclasm provocatively aims to liberate the past from their control, to 'brush the past against the grain' by rethinking it from the point of view of the ruled and the vanquished, not through the eyes of victors."

TRAVERSO'S ESSAY POINTS TO A CRUCIAL REALITY THAT THE "ANTI-woke" media too often overlooks. Campaigners against statues of men such as Rhodes or Lee are not looking to vaporize these monuments or to erase the men they represent from history; rather, they want any public presentation of these figures to be properly contextualized, making clear the complicated motives behind and legacies of their "heroic" actions. It is with this reality in mind that Stanford University historian Priya Satia sought to align Orwell with the BLM movement, and not with those it threatened. In a piece in *Slate*, published that same month and entitled, "What's Really Orwellian about Our Global Black Lives Matter Moment," Satia made clear her belief that Orwell would have been on the side of the BLM protestors, who were seeking to reclaim history, and against the protectors of an imposed history of the winners. "What could be more Orwellian than the proud display of statues of conquerors and slavers in a society continually protesting imperial innocence and devotion to liberty and equality? 'Ignorance is Strength,' the Ministry of Truth would say."

To claim that Black activists are the Orwellian tyrants, and Western civilization their victim, one needs to believe that the economically and socially marginalized Black communities in Western Europe and the United States wield significant power over the mainstream, predominantly white establishment. Would that it were so, some would likely say, but the evidence of the past few years does not bear them out. The statistics on economic disparities between Black and white communities in the US and Britain worsened during the pandemic, driven in large part by pre-existing wealth disparities between the two groups, which left Black families with less of a safety net to weather the economic impact of COVID. France does not differentiate official economic statistics by race, yet scholars have used proxy data to expose similar patterns of disadvantage as in the US and Britain. Statistics on police shootings in the United States, and on stops and arrests in the US, Britain, and Germany, show that racism remains alive and well within Western policing. While, by many metrics, Western society is less racist and more self-aware in its treatment of the legacies of imperialism and slavery than in Orwell's day, the dynamic of oppression has shifted but has not been eradicated, and, from the moment he resigned from the Indian police, Orwell consistently aligned himself with the oppressed.

It is dangerous to put words in the mouth of the dead, and we cannot say with certainty how Orwell would have reacted to witnessing the campaigns waged against statues of imperialists and racists in European and American city squares. In *The Road to Wigan Pier*, he first confesses that, in his twenties, after leaving the Indian police, "I had reduced everything to the simple theory that the oppressed are always right and the oppressors are always wrong," but then goes on to say that this was "a mistaken theory, but the natural result of being one of the oppressors yourself." It's possible that Orwell would have deemed the behavior of the BLM protestors extremist or misguided, but he would certainly have recognized who were the oppressed and who were the oppressors.

ORWELL'S WORK, AND IN PARTICULAR HIS FINAL NOVELS *ANIMAL Farm* and *Nineteen Eighty-Four*, played an enormous role in focusing popular attention on the relationship between political language and political practice. His notion that people could not be truly free in a society where they could not speak their minds offers an important corrective to those who would argue that there is a freedom to be had in trading political liberty for economic or social security. Yet, Orwell's understanding of politics was not limited to a critique of the bastardization of language and the devaluation of truth in ungood (to use a Newspeak term) societies such as Stalinist Russia or Nazi Germany.

Rather, he believed that any society held a potential for tyranny, and that it was important to be vigilant against abuses of power by regimes of all political persuasions, including purported democracies. It is notable in this case that the governing party in *Nineteen Eighty-Four* is Ingsoc at a time when the British Labour government frequently referred to themselves as "socialists" or as the "Socialist Party." Orwell continued to back Attlee's Labour government until his death, and wrote in June 1949 to an American reader that *Nineteen Eighty-Four* "is NOT intended as an attack on Socialism or on the British Labour Party (of which I am a supporter). . . . [Rather,] the book is laid in Britain in order to emphasize that the English-speaking races are *not* innately better than anyone else and that totalitarianism, if not fought against, could triumph anywhere."

3

ISMS

Populism and Tyranny

I first read George Orwell as a twelve-year-old schoolgirl, during the dying days of the Cold War, when *Animal Farm* was considered an ideal vehicle to teach Western students about the perils of Soviet totalitarianism and to inculcate the virtues of America's commitment to free speech and the protection of political dissent. I went on to read *Nineteen Eighty-Four* in high school English, where my teacher made analogies between Big Brother and Joseph Stalin and the cult of personality and spelled out the connections between Newspeak and Room 101 and Soviet censorship and the torture and repression of the Gulag.

Donald Trump Jr. is a year older than I am. Missouri senator Josh Hawley is a year younger. For American children of our generation, as for children throughout the West, the Orwell we were taught in school was a cold warrior, an anti-communist crusader against thought policing and dictatorial repression. If I had left Orwell behind in high school, I can imagine having sympathy for Trump and Hawley's claims, made in the aftermath of the January 6, 2021, uprising, that Orwell, the anti-Stalinist tribune beloved of Reaganite and Thatcher-era school curricula, would have been on their side.

But I didn't leave Orwell behind. In college, I read Orwell's indictments of racial oppression based on his experience as an imperial officer in Burma, and his writings on unemployment and poverty in Britain and France. I read *Homage to Catalonia*, in which Orwell details his bitter disillusionment with the promise of Soviet communism and his realization that, in practice, Stalinism differed little from Nazi fascism. I also gained my first taste of Orwell's journalism, which, to a greater extent than his book-length writings, highlights the dangers to liberty posed by fascist totalitarianism. The image in *Nineteen Eighty-Four* of Big Brother's tyranny as "a boot stamping on a human face—forever" is a clear allusion, not to Stalinism, but to the jackbooted SS officers who tyrannized Jews and the other perceived enemies of the state in Nazi Germany.

Because Orwell valued truth and liberty so highly, he was determined to expose the assault on those values from both the Stalinist totalitarianism of the left and the fascist totalitarianism of the right. He was equally committed to exposing threats to liberty in the purportedly democratic British Empire. As such, Orwell's political writing has particular relevance to our modern moment, not as a defense of far-right populist speech, but as a lens through which to view both totalitarian oppression overseas and, perhaps unexpectedly, exploitation and bigotry at home.

———

THE RISK OF VIEWING ORWELL'S POLITICS EXCLUSIVELY THROUGH the lens of anti-Stalinism—or, as many of his contemporaries and successors wrongly understood it, anti-socialism—is that it masks the extent to which Orwell perceived the will to power as a universal tendency, one that was largely separate from political ideology and could manifest itself in political movements of either the left or the right. In his 1945 essay "Notes on Nationalism," he sketched out a capacious definition of the term, which effectively encompassed all forms of ambitious populism and totalitarianism:

> A nationalist is one who thinks solely, or mainly, in terms of competitive prestige. He may be a positive or a negative nationalist—that is, he may use his mental energy either in boosting or in denigrating—but at any rate his thoughts always turn on victories, defeats, triumphs and humiliations. . . . Nationalism is power hunger tempered by self-deception. Every nationalist is capable of the most flagrant dishonesty, but he is also—since he is conscious of serving something bigger than himself—unshakeably certain of being in the right.

It's a definition that can be applied as easily to right-wing as left-wing ideologies, and Orwell goes on to discuss a wide variety of toxic "nationalisms" operating in modern Britain. These nationalisms—or more aptly "isms," as most had little to do with the nation as we generally conceive it—included, inter alia, Celtic nationalism, class feeling, "colour feeling" (a.k.a. racism), communism, neo-Toryism ("commitment to denying Britain's diminished state in the world"), pacifism, political Catholicism, and Zionism. "Nationalism" is a broad church where all but a few have worshipped, at least on occasion.

Contemporary Russian readers appear to have grasped this

fundamental truth about the nonpartisan nature of Orwell's
political criticism more intuitively than readers in the West. In
December 2022, the TASS news agency announced that *Nineteen
Eighty-Four* was the most popular fiction download from the Russian online bookseller LitRes, and the second most popular title in
any category. *Nineteen Eighty-Four* had been banned in the USSR
until 1988 as a dangerous critique of Soviet totalitarian, although
samizdat editions circulated behind the Iron Curtain throughout the Cold War. Communism is now a thing of the past, but
Putin's regime remains wary of the political message of *Nineteen
Eighty-Four*. The online newspaper the *Moscow Times* (whose site,
in an Orwellian development, was blocked by the Russian state
in April 2022 for its coverage of the Ukraine war), reported that,
while *Nineteen Eighty-Four* in theory has not been banned and
can be distributed freely in Russia, in April 2022, lawyer Anastasia
Rudenko and businessman Dmitry Silin gave out copies of the
novel in Ivanovo, a city to the northeast of Moscow. "But the pair
were detained and charged with discrediting the Russian army,
which is punishable with a jail term of 15 years in prison."

While the book supposedly remains legal in Russia, supporters of the regime have sought to reframe the text as a critique, not
of totalitarianism (or "nationalism"), but of Western liberal deca-
dence. The same month in which the two activists were charged
for distributing copies of *Nineteen Eighty-Four*, a spokeswoman
for Russia's foreign ministry claimed, "For many years we believed
that Orwell described the horrors of totalitarianism. This is one of
the biggest global fakes. . . . Orwell wrote about the end of liberalism. He depicted how liberalism would lead humanity to a dead
end." That same month, Darya Tselovalnikova, who had recently

completed a new translation of the novel for the Russian publishing house AST, claimed that the novel's contemporary relevance lay in its exposure of totalitarian tendencies within Western society: "Orwell could not have dreamt in his worst nightmares that the era of 'liberal totalitarianism' or 'totalitarian liberalism' would come in the West and that people—separate, rather isolated individuals—would behave like a raging herd." Yet, given the coincidence of *Nineteen Eighty-Four*'s surge in popularity with the renewed crackdown on free speech in Russia, its Russian readers presumably recognize the echoes of Big Brother, Ingsoc, and Newspeak in their own country, as much if not more than in the decadent West.

BEYOND EVEN THE DISTORTION AND CENSORSHIP OF LANGUAGE discussed in the previous chapter, Big Brother's regime in *Nineteen Eighty-Four* seeks totalizing control of its citizens' thoughts and actions. Sex is discouraged as an act that cannot be controlled by the state, and the novel's heroine, Julia, is a member of the Anti-Sex League. (Notably, Julia professes to be uninterested in politics, but enacts her personal rebellion against the state through wanton promiscuity. In Oceania, the personal is decidedly political.) Two-way telescreens allow fitness instructors to see into your home and monitor that you are keeping up with your daily regimen of "physical jerks," like sinister Peloton instructors monitoring milestones. Thought Police from the Ministry of Truth are vigilantly on the lookout for deviations from the accepted party line. Nothing is private. The novel's hero, Winston Smith, comes on the radar of the Ministry of Truth for his decision to keep a diary.

Orwell had initially considered entitling his novel *The Last Man in Europe*, suggesting that, in submitting to absolute tyranny, an individual loses their sense of self and, absent consciousness of their own autonomy, they effectively forfeit their humanity.* In such a regime, it is tragic, but unsurprising, that Winston is ultimately defeated, his mind broken. As Orwell wrote in *Tribune* magazine shortly after the war, "The greatest mistake is to imagine that the human being is an autonomous individual. The secret freedom which you can supposedly enjoy under a despotic government is nonsense, because your thoughts are never entirely your own."

In China, the emphasis on not only punishing but eradicating "thought crime" means that the Xi Jinping government is that much closer to realizing the nightmare regime that Orwell named "Eastasia." (Although written in the early days of the Cold War, *Nineteen Eighty-Four* depicts a world divided not between two superpowers, but three: Oceania, comprised of the British Empire and the United States; Eurasia, made up of the Soviet Union and continental Europe; and Eastasia, dominated by China.) Xi's campaign against the Uyghur Muslim community concentrated in the northwest region of Xinjiang is premised on the fear that the Uyghurs' Turkic culture and Muslim religion represent a de facto threat to the regime, as they offer an alternative basis of loyalty and identity to the Chinese Communist Party. The euphemis-

---

* Orwell may well have taken the ultimate title for his final novel from a dystopian poem published by his late wife, Eileen, in 1934. "End of the Century, 1984" posits a near future in which *sun-bronzed scholars tune their thought / To Telepathic Station 9 / From which they know just what they ought: . . . Mental cremation that shall banish / Relics, philosophies and colds— / Mañana-minded ten-year-olds.*

tically termed "re-education camps" in which over one million Uyghurs are reportedly being secretly detained are, according to Western intelligence, effectively little more than sites of torture, rape, and genocide. Yet, President Xi has defended the party's stated goal to "incorporate education about a shared awareness of Chinese nationhood into education for Xinjiang cadres, youth and children, and society." He has claimed that the aim of the camps is to "make a shared awareness of Chinese nationhood take root deep in the soul."

THE UYGHURS ARE BEING PERSECUTED AS AN ETHNIC AND RELIgious minority. Even before the People's Republic, the Han majority had been intent on eradicating Muslim culture and religion, which it viewed as an alternate pillar of authority to the Chinese state. Writing in the 1930s and 1940s, Orwell took a dim view of the role of religion in society; he believed it served principally to delude and divide humanity. Half a century after Nietzsche proclaimed that "God is dead. And we have killed him," the West appeared to be dominated by a cynical secularism. Both Nazism and Bolshevism were brazenly atheist. For all its "spirituality," Nazi antisemitism (like Orwell's own knee-jerk antisemitism, which he strove in his later years to overcome) was driven by racism rather than religion. The Catholic Church still held considerable power, but Orwell perceived Catholicism as effectively little more than a tool of the reactionary propertied classes in Southern Europe. "Political Catholicism" is one of the dangerous "isms" he denounces in his "Notes on Nationalism."

By the time Orwell wrote *Animal Farm*, Stalin had allowed the Orthodox Church to openly resume its activities in Russia, after two decades of persecution. But, rather than representing an alternative locus of cultural power for the Soviet regime during the Great Patriotic War (as World War II is known in Russia), the Orthodox Church supported the war effort by promising the Soviet people hope and comfort. In *Animal Farm*, Orwell uses the character of Moses, the tame raven, to represent the Orthodox Church. During the "bad old days" of Farmer Jones, Moses would hang around the farm, telling the animals tales of Sugarcandy Mountain, a mythical paradise "somewhere up in the sky, a little distance beyond the clouds." "In Sugarcandy Mountain it was Sunday seven days a week, clover was in season all the year round, and lump sugar and linseed cake grew on the hedges." Orwell, himself an agnostic, if not an outright atheist, albeit one with a fondness for the King James Bible and the ritual of the Church of England, claimed, bitingly, that the animals "hated Moses because he told tales and did no work." But some of them believe in Sugarcandy Mountain, and their belief helps to reconcile them to their oppression. In the early days of the revolution, the pigs drive away Moses, fearing that he will undermine support for revolution. Yet, by the novel's end, when the animals are exhausted by constant battle with the neighboring farms and seemingly endless drudgery and are beginning to question whether the revolution is worth it, the pigs quietly allow Moses to return to the farm. The opiate of the masses that Moses is peddling is now a useful tool to reconcile the animals to life under the control of the pigs.

The one place where Orwell did perceive religion to continue to play an independent and outsized role in politics was the Indian subcontinent. In *Burmese Days*, ethnic and religious differences serve to divide the native characters and fuel the Buddhist sub-divisional magistrate U Po Kyin's vendetta against the

Hindi Dr. Veraswami. As in *Animal Farm*, Orwell consistently mocks religion throughout the novel. At one point, a traveling "book-wallah" explains to Flory that he will make a trade for any book, barring the Bible. "'No, sahib,' he would say plaintively, 'no. This book (he would turn it over disapprovingly in his flat brown hands) this book with a black cover and gold letters—this one I cannot take. I know not how it is, but all sahibs are offering me this book, and none are taking it. What can it be that is in this black book? Some evil, undoubtedly.'" Elsewhere, U Po Kyin dismisses his wife's accusation that his sinfulness will have consequences in the form of reincarnation as "a rat, a frog or some other low animal" by assuring her that he was "a good Buddhist and intended to provide against this danger. He would devote his closing years to good works, which would pile up enough merit to outweigh the rest of his life. Probably his good works would take the form of building pagodas." Religion to Orwell is an evil con, and one with the power to cause meaningful harm—a truth that he was convinced would doom Mahatma Gandhi's efforts to unite the subcontinent. One of his very few published comments on the Indo-Pakistani War that followed the region's independence from Britain in 1947 was that Gandhi "had lived just long enough to see his life work in ruins, because India was engaged in a civil war which had always been foreseen as one of the by-products of the transfer of power."

The Indo-Pakistani War of 1947–48 is only one of many ethnic and religiously motivated conflicts to break out in nations that secured their victory from the British Empire after the Second World War. It is a phenomenon that many have attributed to the role of the British in strategically fomenting interethnic and religious rivalries to facilitate their exercise of power.

SERVING IN THE INDIAN POLICE WAS A SIN FOR WHICH ORWELL
was determined to atone, in part through a career dedicated to
exposing the evils of empire and advocating for its abolition. Thus,
in November 1945, when the Tory Duchess of Atholl, a staunch
anti-fascist who had risked her political reputation to advocate
for the Spanish Republicans and against Britain's official policy
of non-intervention in the Spanish Civil War, invited Orwell to
speak at a meeting of the League for European Freedom, Orwell
demurred. The league was a group created to aid displaced persons
seeking to avoid repatriation behind the Iron Curtain, a cause of
which Orwell approved. In a letter to Atholl, Orwell professed to
"hate Russian totalitarianism and its poisonous influence in this
country" as much as the duchess, and owned that "what is said on
your platforms is more truthful than the lying propaganda found
in much of the press." Nonetheless, he wrote, "I cannot associ-
ate myself with an essentially Conservative body which claims to
defend democracy in Europe but has nothing to say about British imperialism. It seems to me that one can only denounce the
crimes now being committed in Poland, Jugoslavia, etc. if one is
equally insistent on ending Britain's unwanted rule in India."

Orwell similarly made his priorities clear in an essay published in the *Adelphi* shortly before the UK joined the war
against Hitler. In it, he criticized the "much discussed" proposals put forth by the *New York Times* journalist Clarence Streit in
his book *Union Now: A Proposal for an Atlantic Federal Union
of the Free*. Streit's seemingly positive proposal for the creation
of an alliance similar to the future North Atlantic Treaty Organization reeked, in Orwell's estimation, of "hypocrisy and self-
righteousness." He encouraged his readers to take a second

look at Streit's list of sheep and goats: "No need to boggle at
the goats (Germany, Italy and Japan). . . . But look at the sheep!
Perhaps the USA will pass inspection if one does not look too
closely. [A big if!] But what about France? What about England?
What about even Belgium and Holland? Like everyone of his
school of thought, Mr Streit has coolly lumped the huge British and French empires—in essence nothing but mechanisms
for exploiting cheap coloured labour—under the heading of
democracies!" Orwell was all for a strong military response to
fascist aggression—after all, he had voluntarily put himself on
the front lines to fight fascism in Spain—but he was unwilling
to accept the pretended moral purity of his own side. In a passing reference to the British Empire, Streit had made clear that,
as India was not "yet fit for self-government, the status quo must
continue." But for Orwell, the empire was a stain on the British
conscience that could not simply be brushed aside.

Orwell's criticism of the empire was not merely that "no modern man, in his heart of hearts, believes that it is right to invade
a foreign country and hold the population down by force." This
was true, but it wasn't the whole story. "Foreign oppression," he
claimed, "is a much more obvious, understandable evil than economic oppression," but the British Empire's oppression of South
Asia was *both* foreign and economic—a truth from which Orwell
never shrank. In his essay denouncing Streit's willful naivete
about the nature of Western democracies, Orwell included a characterization of the evils of the British Empire that merits quoting
at length:

> One gets some idea of the real relationship of England and
> India when one reflects that the per capita annual income in

England is something over £80, and in India about £7. It is quite common for an Indian coolie's leg to be thinner than the average Englishman's arm. And there is nothing racial in this, for well-fed members of the same races are of normal physique; it is due to simple starvation. This is the system which we all live on and which we denounce when there seems to be no danger of its being altered. Of late, however, it has become the first duty of a "good anti-Fascist" to lie about it and help to keep it in being.

This was not the first time that Orwell had made such points in his writing. In *The Road to Wigan Pier*, Orwell had excoriated the supposed anti-imperialism of most members of the British left: "the left-winger continues to feel that he has no moral responsibility for imperialism. He is perfectly ready to accept the products of Empire and to save his soul by sneering at the people who hold the Empire together."

Orwell's sweeping generalization was by no means fair. There were many members of the British left, including the Labour MP Ellen Wilkinson, who did want the empire to disintegrate, even to the extent of supporting the Quit India movement during the Second World War, when the British Empire's loss of India would have had disastrous implications for the war effort. As in much that he writes in *Road to Wigan Pier*, Orwell is exaggerating for effect, but he does not bring up the empire solely to score cheap points against his supposed nemeses within the British left. He wants to make a broader point about the nature of Britain's economic exploitation of the empire: "Under the capitalist system, in order that England may live in comparative comfort, a hundred million Indians must live on the verge of starvation—an evil state

of affairs, but you acquiesce in it every time you step into a taxi or
eat a plate of strawberries and cream. The alternative is to throw
the Empire overboard and reduce England to a cold and unim-
portant little island where we should all have to work very hard
and live mainly on herrings and potatoes."

Orwell returned to the theme of peripheral exploitation and
imperial affluence once again in *Nineteen Eighty-Four*. In a world
whose northern hemisphere was dominated by three superpowers, the Global South became a pawn over which they could fight
for their natural resources, but even more for "a bottomless reserve
of cheap labour. . . . The inhabitants of these areas, reduced more
or less openly to the status of slaves, pass continually from conqueror to conqueror, and are expended like so much coal or oil."
To the peoples of the Global South, Orwell's future dystopia bore
a stark resemblance to their living present as subjects of the British and French empires.

That Orwell advocated home rule and eventual independence
for Britain's colonial possessions despite his conviction that they
were *the* central ingredient in Britain's prosperity tells us an
immense amount about his political priorities. He had no time
for the hypocrisy of many of his contemporaries in failing to own
that the Indian independence to which they professed allegiance
would come with hard costs. In a 1946 essay in *Tribune* magazine,
he urged his readers to face up to the realities implicit in their critique of empire. "If it is really true that our comparative comfort is
simply a product of imperialism, that such things as the Beveridge
Scheme [of universal social security], increased Old Age Pensions,
raising of the school-leaving age, slum clearance, improved health
services and what-not are luxuries which we can only afford if we
have millions of oriental slaves at our command—that, surely, is

a serious consideration." For his own part, he suspected it was at least partly true. It was a difficult position, but one that Orwell was determined to face up to. It is worth remembering as the West debates what Europe and the United States owe, on the one hand, to the Global South, and on the other, to the non-white citizens of their own countries whose presence in those countries can be traced back to the legacies of imperialism and slavery.

WHILE THE FORMAL INSTITUTIONS OF THE WESTERN EUROPEAN empires have been largely dismantled, the global systems of economic exploitation that Orwell condemned remain with us. The cheap fashion industry came of age in Orwell's lifetime, although off-the-rack clothing was initially produced in places like London's East End and New York's Lower East Side by sweatshop laborers who, although horribly exploited, were paid and treated better than the foreign laborers who produced the cotton and silk from which many of the garments were manufactured. Now, much of our clothing is both produced from foreign materials and sewn by foreign labor, with workers across the supply chain paid below subsistence wages in an effort to keep prices low for Western consumers.

Economic imperialism does not only persist as a global phenomenon. According to the Census Bureau, the average annual household income for white Americans in 2019 was just over $76,000 per year. For Black Americans, that figure was just over $46,000, or thirty thousand dollars less. In the United Kingdom, data from the same year gave average white household income as £42,371, compared with £35,526 in Asian households and £25,982 in Black households. This is not the elevenfold differential between British and Indian workers' wages cited by Orwell, but the income and wealth gaps between white and non-white citizens across the West merit greater political attention and action. The existence of a Black underclass in twenty-first-century America is directly traceable to the system of slavery the United States inherited from the British crown. Britain abolished slavery in 1833, and the US at the end of the Civil War. But the racial thinking that had facilitated the slave trade in Britain, its American colonies, and the US for three hundred years did not disappear. In 1848, South Carolina senator John C. Calhoun proclaimed on the Senate floor, "The two great divisions of society are not the rich and poor, but white and black. And all the former, the poor as well as the rich, belong to the upper class, and are respected and treated as equals." Eighty years later, George Orwell would write in *The Road to Wigan Pier*, "In an 'outpost of Empire' like Burma the class-question [among the British] appeared at first sight to have been shelved. There was no obvious class-friction here, because the all-important thing was not whether you had been to one of the right schools but whether your skin was technically white."

The movement for reparations for American slavery that began in earnest following Black author and activist Ta-Nehisi Coates's 2014 essay in the *Atlantic* has in recent years gained considerable strength among Black Americans, even as white Americans from across the political spectrum continue to resist the campaign, or at the least dismiss it as impractical and unrealistic. A 2019 AP-NORC poll found that while seventy-four percent of Black Americans were in favor of government reparations payments to the descendants of enslaved Americans, only fifteen percent of white Americans supported the idea. The failure of the US reparations movement to attract broader support is unsurprising in a political context steeped in backlash against the perceived diminution of white privilege. Donald Trump and other members of the populist right have harnessed fears that America's white working class is losing the status associated with racial privilege that Senator Calhoun identified so many years ago. They have used that fear to fuel not only the MAGA ("Make America Great Again") movement, but also associated campaigns to tighten voting requirements to effectively disenfranchise a number of Black voters and reassert older racial hierarchies. In 2023, Supreme Court justices appointed by Donald Trump struck down affirmative action, which had been portrayed to the white working class and conservative Asian Americans as a strike against them.

IN 2013, CARICOM, AN UMBRELLA ORGANIZATION OF FIFTEEN Caribbean nations, established a commission to investigate the question of reparations in the form of debt relief and international aid from Britain to its member states. Their demands echoed those made in 2003 by then president of Haiti Jean-Bertrand Aristide that France pay Haiti over $21 billion as restitution for the 150 million gold francs' "indemnity" levied against Haiti by the French government as the cost of France acknowledging the former colony's independence in 1825. In a region where annual incomes average below $4,500 per year (in Haiti, below $1,500), reparations, whether via cash payments or via schemes of debt forgiveness that would allow Caribbean nations to focus scarce resources on welfare and development, could make a material difference to the lives of millions.

There is a particular irony, however, to the issue of reparations within the British imperial context, as, following the abolition of slavery in 1833, the British government committed to pay £20 million (roughly £1.25 billion in modern currency) in reparations to the *owners* of slaves in the British Caribbean. One of those slave owners was Charles Blair, Orwell's great-great-grandfather, whose claims against the British state for the manumission of his 359 slaves on two estates in Jamaica amounted to more than £7,000 (equivalent to nearly £500,000 today).

While calls for reparations have not taken center stage in British domestic politics, in recent years the British Black Lives Matter movement has sought to initiate a discussion about the ways in which history continues to be taught in British schools. The movement to "decolonize" British school and university curricula has incited fierce controversy, as discussed in the previous chapter. The question of history curricula may seem academic, especially when compared to the hard facts of income disparities, but as Orwell insisted, history and historical truth matter. As I also brought up in the previous chapter, in making his case for Britain as against the Nazis, he once quipped that the British would "tell fewer lies" if they won the war. Winston Smith, in trying to clarify his reasons for hating Big Brother to Julia, exclaims, "Do you realize that the past, starting from yesterday, has been actually abolished? . . . History has stopped. Nothing exists except an endless present in which the Party is always right." Perhaps the best reparation for the sins of the past that can be hoped for is that we at least own up to the truth of our history.

WRITING THESE PAGES ARGUING THAT ORWELL WAS ON THE SIDE of the angels on the issue of the British Empire, I can almost hear the voices of my undergraduate students screaming out to me that Orwell was a racist, and then buttressing their claims with copious evidence from his work. My students are not wrong, although, judged by the standards of his time, he was comparatively committed to racial equality. While Orwell rejected racism and would not have recognized the characterization of himself as racist, he viewed non-white peoples (and frankly, also, the Latin peoples of Southern Europe) through a lens of racial and cultural prejudice that is difficult to excuse from within the context of the twenty-first century. Orwell's critics have all too frequently misframed the arguments against him, as when sociologist Krishan Kumar asserted in the *Times Literary Supplement* that the Asian characters in *Burmese Days*, as well as in Orwell's most famous essays on empire, "A Hanging" and "Shooting an Elephant," "are the passive victims of their condition and incapable of understanding it, let alone doing much about it." In fact, Burmese functionary U Po Kyin, from whose perspective chunks of the novel are written, is the éminence grise driving all of the action in the novel. But while Orwell did not necessarily depict South Asian natives as passive, he did almost invariably depict them in broadly drawn and largely unsympathetic stereotypes.

"Shooting an Elephant" (1936) is Orwell's semi-fictionalized account of his alleged experience of feeling compelled by the force of social pressure to shoot an elephant that, while in "must," had stamped a native "coolie" to death, but that, at the time of its execution, did not pose a threat. Orwell said he "knew with perfect certainty that I ought not to shoot him," but in the end, he went ahead with it, "solely to avoid looking a fool." In sketching out the scene, Orwell refers to the Burmese he felt had pressured him into shooting the elephant variously as "sneering yellow faces," "evil-spirited little beasts," and "the sea of yellow faces above the garish clothes."

The condemned prisoner in "A Hanging" (1931), Orwell's other famous amalgam of narrative license and memoir, in which he claims to recollect his experience of watching a native man's execution, is granted a precious humanity, but he is again described in stereotypical terms: "He was a Hindu, a puny wisp of a man, with a shaven head and vague liquid eyes. He had a thick, sprouting moustache, absurdly too big for his body, rather like the moustache of a comic man on the films."

The Asians in *Burmese Days* are variously grotesque. U Po Kyin might not be a passive victim, but he is an awful caricature. "He was a man of fifty, so fat that for years he had not risen from his chair without help, and yet shapely and even beautiful in his grossness; for the Burmese do not sag and bulge like white men, but grow fat symmetrically, like fruits swelling." Dr. Veraswami, the only man of honor in the novel, is nonetheless portrayed as a fool. "The doctor was a small, black, plump man with fuzzy hair and round, credulous eyes. . . . [H]e was dressed in a badly fitting white drill suit, with trousers bagging concertina-like over clumsy black boots. His voice was eager and bubbling, with a hissing of the s's." He was a voracious reader, but "liked his books to have what he called a 'moral meaning'"—a marker both of his sincerity and his foolishness. Meanwhile, Ma Hla May, the British protagonist's Burmese mistress, is "like a doll, with her oval, still face the colour of new copper, and her narrow eyes; an outlandish doll and yet a grotesquely beautiful one." She is also amoral. Her parents had sold her to John Flory two years before the opening of the novel, but she doesn't mind her sexual servitude. "It was the idle concubine's life that she loved, and the visits to her village dressed in all her finery, when she could boast of her position as a 'bo-kadaw'—a white man's wife." These three, caricatures as they are, are at least given

distinct identities. Elsewhere in the novel, the Burmese are repeatedly referred to as a "sea of people," a "sea of dark faces," a "sea of
bodies," a "a sea of white muslin backs of women, pink scarves
flung round their shoulders and black hair-cylinders." These were
not the words of a man free of racial prejudice.

In his recent book *Orwell and Empire*, Douglas Kerr, a professor of literature at the University of Hong Kong, repeatedly insists
that Orwell is "not our contemporary." It is easy to imagine him
emphasizing this to his students to quell their urge to "cancel"
Orwell for his unpalatable prejudices. Instead of simply writing
Orwell off, Kerr urges his readers to view the author through the
lens of Orwell's historical moment and seek to "understan[d] how
it was that, for all his undoubted intelligence and thoughtfulness,
he nonetheless felt, believed, and said some things that make us
profoundly uneasy." As Kerr notes, this is what the British sociologist and Black activist Paul Gilroy has done in *After Empire* (2004).
Gilroy does not discount the evidence of Orwell's embedded prejudice, but nonetheless classes him on the side of right, as a man
whose "humanistic outlook . . . is directed sharply against the
injustice and inequality of the Empire's racial domination." Readers can reach their own conclusions as to how to weigh Orwell's
casual racism against his anti-imperial activism.

———

WHILE ORWELL CRITIQUED THE EMPIRE IN WHICH HE WAS BORN
and raised, he was nonetheless a patriot. In a meditation on Orwell
and the natural world, the essayist Rebecca Solnit described Orwell
as a man who "managed both to love Englishness and loathe the
British empire." In her opening pages of *Orwell's Roses*, she quotes
a much-loved line of his: "In the good days when nothing in Wool-

worth's cost over sixpence, one of their best lines was their rose bushes. They were always very young plants, but they came into bloom in their second year, and I don't think I ever had one die on me." The sentence comes from one of his wartime columns in *Tribune*, and was written in response to a letter from a reader who had accused him of being "negative" and "always attacking things." His initial response was to claim, "The fact is that we live in a time when causes for rejoicing are not numerous." But then he checks himself and continues by writing of the "Woolworth's Rose." Woolworth's variety stores were an American import—as a child, I loved our local Woolworth's in Bethesda, Maryland—but the image his essay evokes is quintessentially English.

In contrast to the negative impulses of nationalism, Orwell writes of patriotism as driven by "devotion to a particular place and a particular way of life, which one believes to be the best in the world but has no wish to force upon other people." He argues, "Patriotism is of its nature defensive," in contrast to the aggression behind nationalism. While he was no nationalist, George Orwell, the man who chose as his pen name England's patron saint coupled with an English river, was a deep patriot. He desperately resented that his injuries and ill health prevented him from being able to serve Britain, excepting as an officer in the Home Guard, during the Second World War.

He had no truck with those members of the political left who professed complete disdain for their country, as opposed to an awareness of its strengths and weaknesses. On one level, the rhetoric of right-wing pundits such as Tucker Carlson that Democrats hate America is absurd, but it is based on a real phenomenon within parts of the left—a phenomenon that Orwell recognized and deplored. He was a professed socialist who maintained "a faint feeling of sacrilege not to stand to attention during 'God save the King,'" and who felt something between pity and contempt for "the left-wing intellectuals who are so 'enlightened' that they cannot understand the most ordinary emotions," like those that cause one's heart to "lea[p] at the sight of a Union Jack."

His love for the prosaicness of English life appears over and over in his writing, but nowhere more abundantly than in the opening pages of *The Lion and the Unicorn: Socialism and the English Genius*, which we'll explore in more detail in chapter 6. Here, he describes the experience of returning to England from abroad:

> You have immediately the sensation of breathing a different air. . . . The beer is bitterer, the coins are heavier, the grass is greener, the advertisements are more blatant. The crowds in the big towns, with their mild knobby faces, their bad teeth and gentle manners, are different from a European crowd. . . . The clatter of clogs in the Lancashire mill towns, the to-and-fro of the lorries on the Great North Road, the queues outside the Labour Exchanges, the rattle of pin-tables in the Soho pubs, the old maids hiking to Holy Communion through the mists of the autumn morning—all these are not only fragments, but *characteristic* fragments, of the English scene.

The passage is as poignant a paean to England as Blake's *Jerusalem* or Winston Churchill's wartime speeches.

Yet, he was capable of simultaneously loving his country and acknowledging its faults. In one of his most famous passages, also from *The Lion and the Unicorn*, Orwell describes Britain as a family. Yes, it's "a family in which the young are generally thwarted and most of the power is in the hands of irresponsible uncles and bedridden aunts. Still, it is a family. It has its private language and its common memories, and at the approach of an enemy it closes its ranks." It's a description that many would argue fits the US as well as Britain. Not least, while the US, unlike Britain, has never had a formal empire, it has long been perceived as an imperial power across much of the Global South, which has resented its role as—to use Orwell's terminology in describing the British imperial family—the "source of the family income" for US-owned corporations.

———

ORWELL'S SIMULTANEOUS COMMITMENT TO HOLDING A MIRROR up to his country and to exposing political corruption beyond Britain's borders offers lessons for today. The West, and the United States and United Kingdom in particular, has been quick to denounce Vladimir Putin for his imperial ambitions in Ukraine and beyond and for his domestic repression of any dissent about the war. But leaders in those countries have been slower to interrogate why so many people outside the West, who are not subject to the media blackout that Putin has imposed over his own citizens, appear to be willing to believe Putin's narrative about the Ukraine war. Legacies of US and British imperial action in countries such as Brazil, Cuba, India, and Egypt are still strongly felt. Widespread cynicism about Britain and America's domestic and foreign policy has undermined their global credibility in fights against tyranny abroad. That is not to say that the US and the UK do not have the right, or even the moral imperative, to go after Putin, nor is it to claim a moral equivalency between the West and totalitarian Russia—something that Orwell never suggested in his own time—but rather, to say that the sins of our enemies do not absolve us from our responsibility to own and address our nation's culpability.

It is easy for pundits and politicians to identify and criticize the despotic and totalitarian tendencies of other governments and political movements. It is equally easy to dismiss your own side by saying, "The West is racist," or to write large sections of your compatriots off as "deplorables." It is much more difficult to think critically about the members of your own family. While we can and must stand up against oppressive regimes abroad, we must also take ownership of how and why similar populist and antidemocratic tendencies are corrupting our domestic political systems.

Orwell's journalistic career can serve as a model for conscientious political criticism in our current moment. He chose his side and defended it fervently. At the end of the day, he knew where he stood. As he wrote in 1940, "I was patriotic at heart, would not sabotage or act against my own side, would support the war, would fight in it if possible"—but he never pretended that the battle was black and white.

4

INEQUALITY

Accents and Manners and the Cut of Clothes

In 1999, the movie *Notting Hill*, starring Julia Roberts as an American movie star filming on location in London and Hugh Grant as the diffident bookshop owner with whom Roberts's character falls in love, premiered to international acclaim, grossing $363 million (nearly £200 million) at the box office and securing a European Film Award nomination for best picture. *Notting Hill* was the second collaboration between Grant and writer Richard Curtis, following 1994's *Four Weddings and a Funeral*. In both films, the charmingly foppish Grant is presented as humble and relatable, despite a posh accent and a public-schoolboy demeanor that clearly mark him as being from a more privileged background than the vast majority of the film's viewers. *Notting Hill*'s key romantic moment similarly repurposes a marker of class privilege not as elitist, but as intimate and quaint. The two protagonists climb the fence of one of the many gated private squares in West London, after which the trespassers illicitly kiss among the roses.

In Tony Blair's Britain and Bill Clinton's US when the film premiered, viewers largely accepted Grant's poshness as charming, and West London's secret gardens as innocuous idylls, especially as it was a period of economic and social optimism—that things could only get better, and tomorrow would be better than before. Both politicians and the public gave comparatively little thought to the implications of rising inequality. The important point was that the economic pie was growing, even if it continued to be divided unequally. The rising tide was lifting all ships, though some were buoyed higher than others.

A decade later, in the wake of the Great Recession of 2008, inequality's implications were much more starkly visible. When the bottom fell out of the economy, those without money in the bank were hit hardest by unemployment and falling asset prices, whereas the global elite—the public schoolboys with posh accents and keys to West London gardens—were comparatively insulated.

In 2013, French economist Thomas Piketty published *Capital in the Twenty-First Century*, a rare economic tome to attract reviews in the *New York Times* and the *Guardian*, as well as front-of-store shelf space in Barnes & Noble and Waterstones. In it, he highlighted the trajectory of economic inequality across the West over the past century, revealing that, after a period of comparative equalization between the 1950s and 1970s, inequality in the early twenty-first century had returned to levels not seen since the interwar period. The economic landscape that Piketty surveyed in 2013 looked eerily like the one George Orwell documented in the 1930s. At the time of writing in 2023, the economic impact of high inflation and the spiraling cost of living is once again hitting those at the bottom much harder than those at the top.

But before the crash of 2008, the UK was suspended in a bubble of apparent prosperity, with national growth hiding the widening inequality from view. What would George Orwell have had to say about the world of *Notting Hill*, had he lived to experience it? In one respect, at least, he would have been unequivocally disappointed. Orwell was a vocal opponent of West London's private squares and the iniquitous class privilege that they represented.

Writing in *Tribune* magazine in August 1944, Orwell recapped the story of the removal and replacement of the railings and gates around these private squares. Early in the war, they had been taken away and used as scrap metal as a military expedient that "was also felt to be a democratic gesture," giving people access to these small parks. Orwell believed the removal of the gates to be an unalloyed social good. When, even before Hitler's armies were defeated, wood fencing was put up in place of the iron rails, re-establishing the physical boundary between the rich and the poor, he rued the development: "the lawful denizens of the squares can make use of their treasured keys again, and the children of the poor can be kept out."

Tribune was a left-wing magazine, but to at least one reader, Orwell's comments went too far. "Are the squares to which you refer public or private properties?" the reader enquired. "If private, I suggest that your comments in plain language advocate nothing less than theft and should be classed as such."

Orwell would not be deterred:

If giving the land of England back to the people of England is theft, I am quite happy to call it theft. In his zeal to

defend private property, my correspondent does not stop to
consider how the so-called owners of the land got hold of it.
They simply seized it by force, afterwards hiring lawyers to
provide them with title-deeds.

Such a full-throttled attack on the principle of private property would sound radical coming from the mouth of Jeremy Corbyn, and unimaginable if uttered by Bernie Sanders, or even by
Alexandria Ocasio-Cortez, but Orwell had been radicalized by
his encounters with the effects of massive inequality on British
and colonial society over the previous twenty years. Experience
had made him cynical about capitalism, and more than any kind
of positive utopianism, it had turned him toward socialism as the
only solution for what he perceived as a decadent consumer capitalism in the throes of crisis.

In this sense, he is not dissimilar to Piketty, whose experience documenting the persistence of inequality across the past
century, and its rapid explosion in recent decades, has led him to
embrace a defiant socialism. In 2021, Piketty published *Time for
Socialism: Dispatches from a World on Fire* (in French, *Vivement
le socialisme!*). In its introduction, he noted that, as a student in
the 1990s, he had been an economic liberal, convinced that the
collapse of the Soviet Union proved the failure of socialism, and
that "the market economy and private property were part of the
solution. . . . But now, thirty years later, in 2020, hypercapitalism
has gone much too far." He continued, "I am now convinced that
we need to think of a new way of going beyond capitalism, a new
form of socialism, participative and decentralized, federal and
democratic, ecological, multiracial and feminist." Such a political
revolution could be facilitated by a significant redistribution of

capital through progressive taxation in order to redress the cumu-
lative impacts of generations of inequality. Except perhaps for his
insistence that any socialist solution must be environmentally
conscious and feminist, his ideas would almost certainly have
appealed to Orwell.

It's ironic, and yet one more instance of how misunderstood
Orwell remains, that the author of a *Wall Street Journal* review of
Capital in the Twenty-First Century suggested that Piketty ought to
have read *Animal Farm* and Arthur Koestler's *Darkness at Noon*, a
novel set in the USSR, before daring to propose such socialist solutions to the problem of inequality. Orwell and Koestler, a friend,
were in agreement about the totalitarian perversions of the Stalin
regime, but were equally in agreement about the failure of unbri-
dled capitalism. In 1946, Orwell, Koestler, philosopher Bertrand
Russell, and Victor Gollancz briefly attempted to form a "League
for the Dignity and Rights of Man." Koestler's papers contain a
memorandum from Orwell in which he mused that a key aim of
the group should be to generate a definition of democracy that
went beyond nineteenth-century liberalism of the free-market
kind—which the *Wall Street Journal* continues to embrace—and
that defined "the main function of the state" as being "to guaran-
tee the newborn citizen his equality of chance," and "to protect
him against economic exploitation by individuals or groups."

For Orwell, surveying the political scene in the 1930s and
1940s, the role played by social and economic inequality in undermining democracy and facilitating both political apathy and the
rise of authoritarianism could not be underestimated. In *Nineteen
Eighty-Four*, written in the aftermath of the Second World War,
Orwell included a lengthy "book within a book"—Emmanuel
Goldstein's history of the Party (which may or may not actually

have been written by Goldstein, who in turn may or may not actually exist). Orwell uses "The Book" to extemporize on the nature of power and the mechanisms of tyranny. In it, Orwell, writing as Goldstein, contends that inequality is the cornerstone on which the tyranny of *Nineteen Eighty-Four*, and all past tyrannies, are built. He envisions that a prosperous society would be a more equitable society: "It was possible, no doubt, to imagine a society in which wealth, in the sense of personal possessions and luxuries, should be evenly distributed, while power remained in the hands of a small privileged caste. But in practice such a society could not long remain stable.

Some would argue that Orwell/Goldstein was overly optimistic and that the persistence of social hierarchy even within the wealthiest pockets of the twenty-first century West belies his argument. Yet, even if he was naive in thinking that the universal possession of indoor plumbing, refrigeration, and the automobile would be enough to topple the class system, he was prescient in appreciating the central role of inequality in perpetuating the status quo.

───────

RETURNING TO THE WORLD OF *NOTTING HILL*, BOTH BLAIR AND Clinton have taken criticism from the left in recent years for their failure to tackle rising inequality while in office. In 2022, the American academic Lily Geismer came out with *Left Behind: The Democrats' Failed Attempt to Solve Inequality*, a blistering attack on the Clinton administration's economic policies. In Britain, criticism of the Blair era has not been limited to academics. Members of the party's left wing have vocally denounced Blairism as being, in practice, little different from Toryism.

Both Clinton and Blair have responded with robust defenses of their economic policies, pointing to their successes in combating poverty through such programs and legislation as the implementation of the minimum wage and the child poverty target and the Child Poverty Act in Britain, and the expansion of the earned income tax credit and passage of the State Children's Health Insurance Program in the US. However, Clinton also changed welfare requirements so that they were funded by block grants to states, implemented work requirements, and put limits on the length of time one could receive welfare. Furthermore, their detractors point to the long-term negative impacts of policies such as the Blair government's outsourcing of public services to public-private partnerships that too frequently enriched private providers at the expense of public provision, or the Clinton administration's deregulation of the banking sector, which arguably enabled the Lehman Brothers collapse that precipitated the 2008 recession.

The fiery debates between Blair and Clinton's supporters and detractors speak to a key question that divided the left in Orwell's time and that continues to divide them to this day: Should progressive activists focus exclusively on the elimination of poverty, or does inequality matter?

For Orwell, at least, equality was central to the democratic socialist project as he understood it. He staunchly aligned himself with "the vast majority of people [for whom] Socialism means a classless society, or it means nothing at all." Equality, Orwell claimed, was "the 'mystique' of Socialism"; it was what drew ordinary people to the movement. By exploring inequality through Orwell's eyes, we can perhaps rethink our own understanding of the role it plays within contemporary politics.

———

EQUALITY DOESN'T COME OFF WELL IN *ANIMAL FARM*. THERE,
Orwell presents it as the Big Lie that underpins the despotic regime
of the pigs. "All Animals Are Equal" is the first commandment
of Animalism, painted on the barn wall, but it is an equality in
name only. While the citizens of Animal Farm are putatively free
and equal, power, privilege, and responsibilities are apportioned
unequally among the farm animals to an even greater extent than
they had been when they were ruled by Mr. Jones. By the end of the
novel, the pigs are so secure in their power over the other animals
that they feel able to do away even with this foundational lie. One
night, while the other animals sleep, the pigs quietly amend the
commandment to read, "All animals are equal, but some animals
are more equal than others."

For those who insist on misreading *Animal Farm* as a critique
of socialism writ large, rather than as a critique of the Stalinist
perversion of socialism, the pigs' concluding act merely exposes
the lie that equality is anything more than an unachievable fairy
tale. But, despite his contempt for Stalinism, Orwell remained
committed to the realization of greater social equality.

For Orwell, equality, at least in Britain, was as much about the
absence of social prejudice as about economics. (Although, as we
saw in the previous chapter, Orwell appreciated that the dynamics of imperial exploitation gave racial inequalities a sharper economic edge.) While British income inequality began a sustained
decline in 1914, in the 1930s the wealthiest ten percent of the population still held roughly eighty-five percent of the country's wealth.
Yet, as Orwell well knew, Britain wasn't a country in which wealth
translated directly into social prestige. The two were, undeniably,
intimately linked. However, as we've seen, he was a self-described

member of the "lower-upper-middle class" and intimately aware that it was possible for a person's balance of social capital to significantly exceed their financial capital, and vice versa. For Orwell, social inequalities were as pernicious as income inequalities, as they helped to ensure that British society remained divided into warring castes, and that those members of the lower-middle (and lower-upper-middle) class failed to make common cause with the working classes against the truly exploitative elite—the group that we have come to characterize, since the birth of the Occupy Movement in the early 2000s, as the one percent.

Orwell wrote compassionately and perceptively about the lives of the British working classes. As we'll discuss below, his journalism is notable not only for its clear-eyed discussion of the incomes and living conditions of the urban poor, but also for his understanding of how modern consumer culture shaped the lived experience of interwar poverty in ways which have many echoes in our own twenty-first-century moment. Yet, Orwell's writing is often most perceptive not when he discusses the lives of the working poor, which he could only ever understand from the perspective of an outside observer, but when he dissects the pernicious impact of social stratification on the members of the class in which he was raised.

While there is no clear record of what, if any, passive income his family derived from capital investments, his father's India Office pension alone would have put his family in the top two percent of taxpayers in Edwardian Britain. Yet, in his own retelling, Orwell's awakening to the corrosive force of inequality did not come from an awareness of his unearned privilege, but from a resentment of his comparative deprivation. As mentioned in chapter 1, when Orwell went to St. Cyprian's preparatory school at the age of eight, he was surrounded by a group of boys much wealthier than himself. In his 1947 essay "Such, Such Were the Joys," written through the decidedly non-rose-tinted lens of hindsight, Orwell recreated the social atmosphere of his early days at prep school, which was divided into three "castes." There were "the minority with a millionaire background, there were the children of the ordinary suburban rich, who made up the bulk of the school, and there were a few underlings like myself, the sons of clergyman, Indian civil servants, struggling widows and the like." The social hierarchy was rigidly enforced by both the headmaster and the students. It was an environment in which "all the very rich boys were more or less undisguisedly favoured."

In this environment, Orwell absorbed a new definition of what it meant to be economically successful. "You were no good unless you had £100,000 a year. . . . The interest on £100,000 would be £4,000 a year (I was in favour of a safe 4 percent), and this seemed to me the minimum income that you must possess if you were to belong to the real top crust, the people in the country houses." (For perspective, slightly over twenty thousand British households reported income above £4,000 per annum in 1911, or less than 0.1 percent of the population.) Orwell knew he would never attain such wealth, but, as a child, it didn't occur to him to reflect on whether the fact that some of his classmates were so ostentatiously wealthy was itself socially problematic, rather than merely enviable. As he relates, "Before the [First World War] the worship of money was entirely unreflecting and untroubled by any pang of conscience. The goodness of money was as unmistakable as the goodness of health or beauty, and a glittering car, a title or a horde of servants was mixed up in people's minds with the idea of actual moral virtue."

As a blanket statement, this is obviously not true. The fin de siècle saw the birth of socialist movements across Europe and America, with the founding of the Independent Labour Party in Britain in 1893 by the Scottish miner-turned-trade union leader Keir Hardie, and the formation of the International Workers of the World, or "Wobblies," a self-professed "revolutionary industrial union," in 1905. France's current Socialist Party, for decades one of the two parties dominating elections and the government, was born out of this turn. In the US, the Socialist Party of America was founded in 1901, and in 1912 its presidential candidate, Eugene V. Debs secured six percent of the vote. All these movements calling for a radical redistribution of resources from capital to labor did so in moral language that depicted the concentration of capital in the hands of the few as decidedly unvirtuous. Socialists who were religious, such as John Malcolm Ludlow in Britain and followers of the Social Gospel movement within American Protestantism, decried the gross inequality of fin de siècle plutocratic society and campaigned for fundamental social reform in Christ's name.

Nevertheless, the future George Orwell did not notice this critique on class, felt surrounded by a group of "intimately, intelligently snobbish" peers, and developed a hyperconsciousness of status distinctions—an ability "to detect small difference in accents and manners and the cut of clothes"—that was to define his writing on class and equality throughout his career.

Orwell's writing on his childhood is filled with unironic references to his family's sense of comparative disadvantage. Families like his own, he contended, had "far more *consciousness* of poverty than in any working-class family above the level of the dole. Rent and clothes and school-bills are an unending nightmare. . . . Practically the whole family income goes in keeping up appearances."

On one level, this sounds patently absurd. Why should anyone feel sympathy for their plight when they were a long way from poverty? Yet, the Blairs were not dissimilar from the squeezed middle classes (really the squeezed upper-middle classes) that Elizabeth Warren profiled in *The Two-Income Trap*, the book that won her a professorship at Harvard Law School and set her on the path to serving as Massachusetts's senior senator.

In *The Two-Income Trap*, Warren and her daughter, Amelia Warren Tyagi, study the economic pressures that have pushed middle-class mothers into the workforce. The principal pressure, they contend, is the spiraling cost of a family home in a good school district: "As parents increasingly believe that the differences among schools will translate into differences in lifetime chances, they are doing everything they can to buy their way into the best public schools. Schools in middle-class neighborhoods may be labeled 'public,' but parents have paid for tuition by purchasing a $175,000 home within a carefully selected school district." Warren and Tyagi wrote their book two decades ago. House prices have only continued to spiral upward in the intervening years, driven in no small part by the bidding wars for property in "desirable" neighborhoods that the authors cite. Such a situation leaves families spending more of their income on housing, with less of a financial cushion, and precariously exposed to the consequences of one partner losing their job.

While buying your way into the best school district is frequently presented as an American phenomenon, similar practices abound in the UK. When my sons and I were living in York, where my husband teaches, every parent and estate agent knew the Ofsted (Office for Standards in Education, Children's Services and Skills) ratings of each school in a property's catchment area, and homes were priced accordingly. A colleague, then based in Liverpool, once told me that if he or his wife ever took a job in London, they would move to West London and mortgage themselves to the hilt to get their son into the catchment area for a particular grammar school.

In the Britain of 1911, by contrast, children were merely required to attend school until age eleven, and only an estimated eight percent of fourteen- and fifteen-year-olds, and *two* percent of sixteen- and seventeen-year-olds, remained in schooling. But Orwell and his sisters were part of that tiny minority who not only went to school, but went to private boarding schools. Even with Orwell's half-scholarship at St. Cyprian's, their education bills must have consumed nearly half of the family income. That said, half of an income of £438 per annum still left a lot of income for non-educational expenses. The reality that the Blairs, after school fees, still retained a disposable income between that of a manager and a member of the higher professions undercuts Orwell's characterization of his family as "shabby genteel."

What is more significant than the reality of Orwell's lower-upper-middle-class privilege is the fact that he, and presumably his parents, perceived themselves to be so economically overstretched and comparatively disadvantaged. It is a form of cognitive dissonance that persists today. In 2017, Richard Reeves of the Brookings Institute wrote a scathing exposé of a group that he termed the "dreamhoarders," arguing that a pernicious Orwellian "double-think" among upper-middle-class Americans (a group to which he himself belongs) allows them to believe that they have earned their privilege, even as they pursue unmeritocratic stratagems, such as private schools or mortgaging their way into elite public school districts, to ensure that their children retain their elite class status. A similar process of "double-think" under-pinned President Biden's 2018 campaign pledge that he would not raise taxes on those earning below $400,000 a year—a pledge that effectively included families with incomes in the top two percent of US earners among the squeezed middle classes who should not be asked to contribute more to the commonweal.

None of the above suggests that Orwell was anything other than deeply deluded (and offensive) in his perception that his family was analogous to "a family of 'poor whites' living in a street where everyone else is a Negro. In such circumstances you have got to cling to your gentility because it is the only thing you have." It does, however, suggest that Orwell was not alone in his delusion, and that a clear-eyed recognition of how members of the economic elite can understand themselves as disadvantaged or as the under-dog remains crucial to redressing the deep-rooted inequities that, despite the social democratic reforms of the mid-twentieth cen-tury, have continued to plague our society since Orwell's time.

WHILE THE ADULT ORWELL WROTE VIVIDLY OF HIS CHILDHOOD feelings of social and economic exclusion, his empathy lay with those much closer to the bottom of the social hierarchy. In *The Road to Wigan Pier*, he presents the key to his transformation from "poor little rich boy" to social critic as his time spent in Burma, during which he finally, it seems, came to grips with the sheer extent of his own privilege and the exploitation of others implicit in it. As is so often the case with Orwell, he manages to describe his belated social awakening in terms that disarm with the hon-esty of their self-criticism. Thus, he candidly admits that it was not until his return from Burma that he even was "really aware of the

working class, and to begin with it was only because they supplied
an analogy. They were the symbolic victims of injustice, playing
the same part in England as the Burmese played in Burma." (Specifically, the victims of injustice whose cause Orwell allied himself
with on his return from Burma were the white British masses.
Orwell lived at a time when the non-white population of the British Isles counted fewer than ten thousand people, concentrated
mainly in port cities. Hence, while Orwell remained deeply concerned about the plight of British imperial subjects abroad, he
showed little awareness of the existence of non-white communities in Britain.)

Orwell embarked on an attempt to expiate his sins and to
do penance for his complicity in the British imperial system by
slumming it among London's homeless, tramping across the
south of England with a crew of Cockneys, Irish, and down-on-
their-lucks and gathering material for what became his first book
of nonfiction, *Down and Out in Paris and London*. He combined
his lightly fictionalized reportage of life on the London streets
with a similarly massaged memoir of his time spent in Paris prior
to his London exploits, living in a garret in the Latin Quarter,
trying to become a professional writer and making ends meet
first as a poorly paid tutor and later as a dishwasher at a series of
Parisian restaurants.

If *Down and Out* represented the beginning and end of Orwell's
forays into social investigation, it is unlikely we would still be taking him seriously as a critic of the British class system. From a
twenty-first-century perspective, it is a self-indulgent project. A
man who, by his own admission, had little actual sense of who the
working class were, seeks to assuage his guilt at his own privilege
by living among, not the actual working poor, but the most abject

members of society, an act which he admitted was inspired in part by the work of the American naturalist writer Jack London. He convinces himself that they accept him for who he is, despite his Etonian accent, which he claims, implausibly, few take note of on the road, and that they don't see something creepy about his tramping and skiving with the urban destitute under false pretenses as a form of social investigation. Then he writes a book about it, using a nom de plume so as not to embarrass his respectable middle-class parents and sister in Southwold, with whom he lived while writing the book.

As his friend V. S. Pritchett noted, "He hated being the ruler, he wanted to be (for a while) the victim and the ruled . . . Orwell's revolt may have been dreary to the reader, but for the consuming curiosity of his eyes." Fortunately for posterity, Orwell matured beyond *Down and Out*. In 1936, he headed north from London (where he moved in 1934) to the industrial town of Wigan, not to disguise himself as a northern tramp, but to earn his commission as a journalist, rent lodgings in a working-class community, and document the lives of the northern working poor and unemployed. The result, *The Road to Wigan Pier*, represents one of the most insightful analyses of the impact of poverty on Britain's working classes and the ways in which comparative social disadvantage compounds economic disadvantage to exacerbate inequality. He also shows a clearer understanding than in his earlier writing of the ways in which his own upbringing had and continued to create privilege for him.

In documenting the lives of Wigan's unemployed, Orwell is conscious that many of his readers harbor unrealistic prejudices about the "undeserving poor"—prejudices that have echoed through the decades in denunciations of so-called "welfare queens" in 1980s America, or benefit scroungers in 2010s Britain. "The notion that the working class have been absurdly pampered, hopelessly demoralized by doles, old age pensions, free education, etc., is still widely held," he wrote. In place of these stereotypes, Orwell drew a picture of the working classes that emphasized in vivid detail, not only the horrors of unemployment, but the dangerous conditions of work, poor pay, and the uncertainty that characterized the lives of the working poor.

While *The Road to Wigan Pier* is a grim read, it cannot be classed as voyeurism or poverty porn. The poor's lives were not entirely bleak, and Orwell never pretended that they were. Interwar Britain, he acknowledged, was a wealthy country, in which no one actually starved to death. Theirs was a life where even the poor had access to the comforts of capitalism. "Cheap luxuries"— junk food, radios (the satellite television and smartphones of their day), the cinema, and trendy off-the-rack fashion—kept the working classes of the 1920s and 1930s from recognizing the extent of their comparative disadvantage. Orwell himself didn't like the radio, despite going to work for the BBC during the Second World War. Nonetheless, he appreciated the escapist value of the wireless and the cinema. In 1930s Britain, two-thirds of working-class households owned a radio, and cinema attendance in England averaged between eighteen and nineteen million a week (out of a population of forty million). Compare those figures to the current statistics on subscription television and video streaming services like Sky, Netflix, or HBO. According to Nielsen Media Research, nearly eighty-five percent of Americans, and nearly seventy percent of Britons, use at least one of these. While wellness blogs and upmarket spas encourage users to "disconnect" from technology, for millions, streaming media offers a mechanism of escape similar to an evening spent at the cinema in the 1930s.

Orwell astutely acknowledged the ways in which these consumer "palliatives" dulled the impetus for social revolt. "You may have three halfpence in your pocket and not a prospect in the world, and only the corner of a leaky bedroom to go home to; but in your new clothes you can stand on the street corner, indulging in a private daydream of yourself as Clark Gable or Greta Garbo, which compensates you for a great deal." In that sense, cheap fashion was a tool of oppression: "Whole sections of the working class who have been plundered of all they really need are being compensated, in part, by cheap luxuries which mitigate the surface of life."

The interwar years saw the beginning of a trend that would reach its apex half a century later with the rise of "fast fashion" brands like H&M, Topshop, and Zara.

ORWELL'S ANALYSIS OF THE WAY THAT INCOME INEQUALITY affected spending choices extended beyond leisure to diet, and there he incorporated a similar sensitivity to the ways in which culture and desire impacted consumer choice. It's an analysis with particular relevance to our current moment, in which obesity in the West is increasingly linked with income and perceived by many to be a sign of moral failing. Orwell begins his discussion of working-class diets with reference to journalistic reports of how a family living on unemployment assistance could theoretically put together a grocery list within their budget. It is the kind of thought experiment to which Orwell, the dedicated enumerator, was particularly drawn.

An unemployed worker in 1936 drew a "dole" from the Public

Assistance Committee of thirty-two shillings per week. According to a correspondent in the *New Statesman*, a person could manage on it by spending just under four shillings a week on the following healthy diet: three wholemeal loaves; half a pound of margarine; half a pound of dripping [beef fat]; one pound of cheese; one pound of onions; one pound of carrots; one pound of broken biscuits; two pounds of dates; one can of evaporated milk; and ten oranges. Orwell shows serious skepticism over whether an individual could subsist on such a diet, particularly if they lacked the budget to pay for the fuel with which to cook their raw ingredients (the correspondent, an alleged working man, claimed that he consumed his diet raw to save on fuel expenses). He found this proposed diet not only biologically unrealistic, but also unreflective of actual human eating habits. In contrast to the *New Statesman*'s budget, which Orwell hypothesized might have been a hoax, he noted that a typical unemployed family he had met on his journeys through the north of England spent "only tenpence a week on green vegetables and tenpence half-penny on milk (remember that one of them is a child less than three years old), and nothing on fruit; but they spend one and nine on sugar (about eight pounds of sugar, that is) and a shilling on tea. The half-crown [that they spent] on meat *might* represent a small joint and the materials for a stew; probably as often as not it would represent four or five tins of bully beef. The basis of their diet, therefore, is white bread and margarine, corned beef, sugared tea, and potatoes—an appalling diet."

"Would it not be better," Orwell asked his readers, "if they spent more money on wholesome things like oranges and wholemeal bread or if they even, like the writer of the letter to the *New Statesman*, saved on fuel and ate their carrots raw?" He wasn't just being facetious. Orwell and his wife, Eileen, smoked like two chimneys, but they were exceptionally healthy eaters. Most of the food that they consumed while living at their cottage in Wallington in Hertfordshire was unprocessed and homegrown. Apples and vegetables from their garden, eggs and chickens from their henhouse, and fresh goat's milk to drink. The couple even ran a small shop from their cottage, selling their surplus produce to village neighbors.

But Orwell was not sanctimonious about healthy eating; he appreciated the social pressures that prevented many members of the working class from opting for a healthier diet: "The peculiar evil is this, that the less money you have, the less inclined you feel to spend it on wholesome food. A millionaire may enjoy breakfasting off orange juice and Ryvita biscuits; an unemployed man doesn't. . . . When you are unemployed, which is to say when you are underfed, harassed, bored, and miserable, you don't *want* to eat dull wholesome food. You want something a little bit 'tasty'. . . . Unemployment is an endless misery that has got to be constantly palliated" by the likes of a "two-penny ice-cream," a cup of tea, or "three penny worth of chips."

As Orwell appreciated, the working classes did not have such unhealthy diets simply because they could not afford to eat healthier food (although cost constraints were a real factor), nor because they were ignorant of nutrition. Rather, their diet was a product of both their pocketbooks and their social circumstances. Activists like the English celebrity chef Jamie Oliver or the actress cum lifestyle guru Gwyneth Paltrow would do well to read *The Road to Wigan Pier* before resorting to lecturing the poor on healthier eating habits. When, in 2015, Paltrow took up the challenge of living for a week on the average food budget of the American poor—

$29 in credits from the US government's Supplemental Nutrition Assistance Program (better known as food stamps)—she was confident that she could do so more healthfully than most. She came home from the grocery store with a dozen eggs, a head of lettuce, a bunch of kale, an ear of corn, a single tomato, an avocado, an onion, scallions, frozen peas, a bag of brown rice, tortillas and black beans, cilantro, and seven limes—a bizarre food basket. Presumably she was planning to subsist on vegetarian tacos. Paltrow lasted four days before giving up and purchasing chicken and, crucially, black licorice candy. Not even the Goop guru could survive without some sugar.

The blowback against Paltrow's condescending, yet failed, experiment approximated that experienced by Jamie Oliver two years earlier. In 2013, Oliver came out with a TV show titled *Jamie's Money Saving Meals* and an accompanying cookbook, *Save with Jamie*. In an interview with the *Radio Times* touting the program, Oliver opined about the poor eating habits of Britain's working poor: "I'm not judgmental, but, I've spent a lot of time in poor communities, and I find it quite hard to talk about modern-day poverty. You might remember that scene in [Oliver's previous TV series] *Ministry of Food*, with the mum and the kid eating chips and cheese out of Styrofoam containers, and behind them is a massive fucking TV. It just didn't weigh up." The backlash against Oliver's comments was intense, including in the *Guardian*, where frequent columnist Alex Andreou related what he had learned about eating on a budget during a dark period in his life when he was rendered temporarily homeless:

> What I had not understood before I found myself in true
> poverty, and what Oliver probably does not, is that it means

living in a world of "no." Ninety-nine per cent of what you need is answered "no." Ninety-nine per cent of what your kids ask for is answered "no." Ninety-nine per cent of life is answered "no." Cinema? No. Night out? No. New shoes? No. Birthday? No. So, if the only indulgence that is viable, that is within budget, that will not mean you have to walk to work, is a Styrofoam container of cheesy chips, the answer is a thunderous "YES."

Andreou's observation is effectively the same one that Orwell made a century earlier. Notably Andreou, like Orwell, was a member of the middle class whose temporary sojourn in poverty had given him a consciousness of the working-class mentality that he might not have had had he been born into precarity.

Recognizing the emotional impulse behind poor dietary habits is not the same as endorsing those habits, which Orwell certainly did not. And yet, he felt torn over what, if anything, to do about it. Later in the same chapter of *Road to Wigan Pier*, he related his ambivalence about reports that "[i]n some districts efforts are now being made to teach the unemployed more about food-values and more about the intelligent spending of money":

When you hear of a thing like this you feel yourself torn both ways. . . . First you condemn a family to live on thirty shillings a week, and then you have the damned impertinence to tell them how they are to spend their money. . . . Yet all the same it is a pity that, merely for the lack of a proper tradition, people should pour muck like tinned milk down their throats and not even know that it is inferior to the product of the cow.

The questions of whether and how the state should involve itself in teaching the poor how to eat more healthily has re-emerged as a hot button issue in many Western countries over the past few years. During her husband's time as president, First Lady Michelle Obama attempted to promote healthy eating without the condescension shown by the likes of Oliver and Paltrow. The First Lady, herself an exercise and diet obsessive, avoided criticism of working-class diets, and instead modeled good eating practices through her White House vegetable garden. She worked behind the scenes to improve the dietary offerings in school lunches, with the result that schools across the country began serving whole-grain pasta, breads, and pizza, and adding more fruits and vegetables to their offerings. Large restaurant chains like Olive Garden and Red Lobster added fruits and vegetables in place of french fries on kids' menus; and Walmart cut back on sodium in its packaged foods. Obama's campaign won plaudits, but also detractors. During his presidential run in 2016, Texas senator Ted Cruz promised, "When [my wife] Heidi's first lady, french fries are coming back to the cafeteria!" which played into his supporters' resentment of the supposed nanny state as well as their love of something "tasty."

In the 2020s in Britain, proposals were introduced to ban buy-one-get-one-free deals on products high in fat, sugar, and salt (HFSS), but these were ultimately abandoned in the face of intense backlash from producers and consumers who argued that the scheme, which formed part of a larger anti-obesity campaign, unfairly penalized the poor. Proposed sin taxes on sugar-sweetened sodas in New York State, Chicago, and other US jurisdictions met with the same fate, although similar laws have made it onto the books in Philadelphia and Berkeley, California.

(When the Chicago legislation failed, the conservative *National Review* crowed, "Elites who disparage the guilty pleasures of the rest of society think they are doing everyone a service by stopping unhealthy behaviors . . . [but voters] are fed up with being told how to live by intellectuals.") Despite opposition, the UK's Conservative government imposed a national tax on sugary drinks in 2018, joining France, which began taxing them in 2012, and Mexico, which initiated a similar tax in 2014. More recently, the UK banned the display of HFSS products in prominent supermarket locations such as the ends of aisles and near checkouts. As with earlier battles over sin taxes and health labels on nicotine products, public health arguments ultimately won out over arguments about personal liberty.

The craving for sugar as a palliative for an otherwise grim existence is not, of course, the only—or even the primary—reason that the urban poor make unhealthy dietary decisions. The existence of food deserts—neighborhoods without convenient grocery stores and access to fresh produce—in many urban areas is also a major contributor to poor dietary choices, and policymakers in cities such as Washington, DC, have begun thinking strategically about how to entice grocery stores into underserved communities. Such initiatives acknowledge that poor dietary choices are not just about ignorance or prejudice. While Orwell and Eileen had the luxury of growing their own vegetables and keeping their own goats, most of their working-class contemporaries lacked the facility even to buy goat's milk.

Similarly, advocates for the nutritional benefits of breastfeeding over bottle-feeding are increasingly moving away from simplistic exhortations of "breast is best" to a more nuanced appreciation of the structural barriers that prevent poor working women across

much of the West from nursing their infants. In 2013, a working group of the American College of Obstetricians and Gynecologists issued an opinion that its practitioners should show an
awareness of "the intersecting barriers to breastfeeding that parents may face," and that "Obstetrician–gynecologists and other
health care professionals should strongly advocate for policies that
enable breastfeeding, including paid parental leave and break time
for persons to express milk in the workplace." Orwell's recognition that the problem of poor diets among the urban poor could
not be solved simply by admonishing or educating the working
class, but needed to take into account the social impetus behind
unhealthy eating, remains a valuable lesson for our own day.

YET ANOTHER OFTEN-OVERLOOKED CULTURAL INEQUITY
between the poor and the middle classes that Orwell highlighted
in his work was access to credit and the social protections that
come with it. As he notes in *Road to Wigan Pier*, "Even when I am
on the verge of starvation I have certain rights attaching to my
bourgeois status. I do not earn much more than a miner earns,
but I do at least get it paid into my bank in a gentlemanly manner
and can draw it out when I choose." The working-class miner, by
contrast, was relegated to the cash economy, with all its associated
indignities. In Orwell's novel *A Clergyman's Daughter*, the titular
clergyman is in debt to the butcher, the baker, and every other
tradesman in the town. Although he comes into money, he doesn't
bother to pay off his debts, but invests it in the stock market, much
to his daughter Dorothy's mortification. When she suggests that
the butcher is angry about the outstanding bill and that she can't
blame him for it, her father explodes. "I most certainly can blame

him! . . . That is the kind of thing that we are exposed to in this delightful century. That is democracy—PROGRESS, as they are pleased to call it." The rector took his entitlement to a hefty line of credit with the butcher for granted, whereas his charwoman or the village farm laborers could not rely on the same latitude in paying their debts.

Privilege bred entitlement, which in turn reinforced privilege. The working-class man, Orwell observed, was routinely forced into a "passive role. He does not act, he is acted upon," whereas "a person of bourgeois origin goes through life with some expectation of getting what he wants, within reasonable limits." Nowhere was this sense of passivity and fatalism more clearly visible than in the housing market, which Orwell describes in vivid detail in *The Road to Wigan Pier*. The conditions of slum housing in Wigan and Barnsley were so dire that Gollancz included several photographs in the publication to ensure that they were not accused of libel. Orwell begins his discussion of housing by emphasizing the real implications of the shortage of affordable housing for working people. He pointed out that there was plenty of housing for those who had high incomes. The real problem was the limited supply of decent and affordable working-class housing. That lack meant that "people will put up with anything—any hole and corner slum, any misery of bugs and rotting floors and cracking walls, any extortion of skinflint landlords and blackmailing agents—simply to get a roof over their heads. I have been into appalling houses, houses in which I would not live a week if you paid me, and found that the tenants had been there twenty and thirty years and only hoped they might have the luck to die there."

Years after reading these visceral descriptions of 1930s slum housing, I picked up Matthew Desmond's *Evicted: Poverty and*

Profit in the American City, on the vulnerable communities living in, and frequently being evicted from, slum housing in 2010s Milwaukee, and was taken back to *Wigan Pier*. Desmond vividly describes the fetid conditions tolerated by tenants in Milwaukee's slums. In one example, he notes:

> "Fixing it" often meant getting on without it. The sink was the first thing to get stopped up. After it stayed that way for days, Ruby and Patrice took to washing their dishes in the bathtub. But they weren't able to catch all the foodstuffs from going down the drain and pretty soon concrete-colored water was collecting in the bathtub too. So the family began boiling water on the kitchen stove and taking sponge baths. Afterward, someone would dump the pot water down the toilet and grab the plunger, causing a small colony of roaches to scamper to another hiding spot.

The situation in Milwaukee is by no means unique, either to that city or to the United States. In cities like Dublin and Paris, the lack of available housing stock has long been exploited by unscrupulous landlords. In Britain, such practices are often referred to as "Rachmanism," in reference to the notorious Notting Hill slumlord Peter Rachman, known for exploiting his tenants in the 1950s—a testament to the enduring history of such abuses. Governments have long sought to legislate against landlords' abuses, but tenants' economic precarity and lack of options continue to compel them to tolerate living in subhuman squalor.

In Orwell's estimation, from looking at the working classes in England, generations of passivity and fatalism about their circumstances had bred apathy and complacency that worked against the hope of socialist revolution. Had he taken a broader perspective, he might have considered that resentment of their enforced passivity had been equally instrumental in fueling support for demagogic leaders in countries such as Italy, Germany, and Russia. Orwell hoped that those who had been oppressed by the British class system would one day be awakened to the need for social solidarity and positive revolutionary change. As he wrote in *Nineteen Eighty-Four*, "If there was hope, it must lie in the proles." But, as we saw in the 1930s, and as we have seen recently in right-wing populist movements in the US, Britain, Hungary, Brazil, and beyond, it is equally possible for feelings of resentment and dispossession to be harnessed by those on the right as on the left.

Finally, while this chapter has focused on class inequalities, and particularly the social stratification of male heads of household, it is worth recalling that in 1930s Britain, as today, men make up slightly less than half of the population. In his writing on inequality, Orwell largely ignored the plight of working-class women, many of whom were the principal, if not the sole, breadwinners for their families in the 1930s. In her 1985 book *Wigan Pier Revisited*, Beatrix Campbell asks us to consider how Orwell's picture of 1930s Wigan would have looked if he had focused on female mill workers rather than male miners as the archetypal representative of the working classes in North West England. Then, as now, working-class women suffered from a dual system of patriarchal oppression and financial inequality, and both their lived experience and their politics are defined by the intersection of their gender and racial identities. Yet, Orwell does not give serious consideration to the experience of working-class women, either in *The Road to Wigan Pier* or in his other works. Where he does discuss women, it is almost exclusively in the context of their sexuality, and their politics are presumed to be either nonexistent or instinctively reactionary. If hope lies in the proles, it does not lie for him in the millions of female proles.

5

PATRIARCHY

The Vote, Equal Pay,
and Reproductive Rights

When Orwell thought about the crisis of capitalism, he understood that crisis in classed, not gendered, terms. What he perceived less clearly, if at all, was that the existing patriarchal system had also reached a point of crisis and was equally in need of revolution. He was not alone in privileging class over gender inequality. Many progressive feminists of Orwell's generation resented the marginalization of feminism within left-wing political movements. Many progressive feminists today also harbor similar resentments. And the contradictions between socialism and feminism that impeded progress on gender relations in Orwell's time continue to act as a roadblock to gender equality in ours.

THE ROAD TO WIGAN PIER'S MOST FAMOUS (OR RATHER INFAMOUS) line doesn't concern miners or North West housing estates, but is a denunciation of the "cranks" Orwell believed were within the ranks of the socialist movement. The passage is extraordinary in its prejudice, even for the time in which it was written, condemning the movement for seemingly attracting "every fruit-juice drinker, nudist, sandal-wearer, sex-maniac, Quaker, 'Nature Cure' quack, pacifist, and feminist in England." Even at the time, the inclusion of feminists on Orwell's crank list was, at best, provocative.

This was not the 1970s, when there was a caricatured and tiny number of radical feminists living in lesbian communes, some worshipping Earth goddesses, rejecting the structures of patriarchal capitalism, and deriding and being derided by political conservatives. With the disappearance of the suffragettes following the outbreak of the First World War, there were few radical feminists of any stripe in the 1930s for Orwell to know and condemn. The average feminist in 1930s Britain—like her counterparts in the United States and elsewhere—was not an extremist, nor beyond the political pale. While interwar feminists were deeply committed to achieving social and political change, they eschewed the violent, socially disruptive tactics of the pre-WWI suffragette movement. Rather, they sought to reform society through reasoned argument, acting through organizations such as Britain's National Union of Societies for Equal Citizenship, which campaigned for equal rights for women in the professions and the recognition of women's domestic labor by the state. Many British interwar feminists had a subscription to the feminist periodical *Time & Tide*, which debated birth control, marriage, and women's work and for which, ironically, Orwell wrote theater reviews in the 1940s. An interwar feminist might have cut her hair short in an "Eton crop" in a symbolic strike against the patriarchy. She might even, if she were truly avant garde, have decided to keep her own name after marriage, like the sexologist Marie Stopes, or the Labour MP Dr. Edith Summerskill. While many dismissed her social and political claims as unnatural or imprudent, few would have gone so far as to consider a feminist a crank.

That Orwell, the soi-disant socialist, did so is telling both of his personal politics and of the tension between socialism and feminism still seen today within the US Democratic Party between feminists and "Bernie Bros"; the failure to date of the British Labour Party to elect a woman leader; the hesitancy of many Democrats until recently to use the word *abortion* (preferring for many years to speak euphemistically of a "woman's right to choose"); the initial failure of the Labour Whip's Office to act on sexual misconduct allegations against Swansea West MP Geraint Davies in 2023, or the 2013 allegations of rape and sexual misconduct within the Socialist Workers Party, the left-wing faction within the British socialist left.

The writer Christopher Hitchens, who died in 2011, had been a member of the Socialist Workers Party and had done his best to rescue his literary hero from decades of feminist criticism in his 2002 tribute *Why Orwell Matters*. He argued that while Orwell could be a jaw-droppingly sexist defender of the patriarchy who "suspected that the war between the sexes was an unalterable feature of the natural order, . . . [a]t least it can be said for Orwell that he registered his participation in this unending conflict with a decent minimum of hypocrisy." There are few better examples of damnation by faint praise.

This chapter is not concerned with delving into Orwell's psychological depths to unearth whether his childhood or his experiences in Burma led to his chauvinism—for Orwell was indisputably a chauvinist, even by the standards of his time. Rather, I am interested in exploring what his writing reveals about his gender politics and that of many other members of the progressive left coalition in the interwar decades, and how far Western society has or has not traveled in terms of gender relations over the past eighty years. If Orwell was an author almost singularly committed to speaking the truth, the truth that his writing reveals about the limits of progress in gender relations in the 1930s is discouraging.

———

IN THE 1980S, A GROUP OF FEMINIST SCHOLARS, INCLUDING DEIDRE Beddoe, Beatrix Campbell, and most prominently Daphne Patai in her book *The Orwell Mystique*, extensively dissected what Patai refers to, within Orwell's writing, as androcentrism—his tendency to privilege masculine interests and exclude feminine voices and perspectives, as well as his regular recourse to unflattering stereotypes in creating his female characters. Beddoe's critique of Orwell as a man who had "little or no understanding of the role and predicament of women in the society in which he lived . . . [and whose] awareness of class divisions in society went alongside his lack of understanding of gender divisions" stands the test of time. Yet, while 1980s feminist readings of Orwell were astute in dissecting the author's blindness to gender politics, they devoted comparatively less attention to how his writing reflected on the sexual politics of his era. This is particularly true in regards to both Orwell's writing on birth control and abortion and to the normalization of male sexual predation and aggression in Orwell's fiction and nonfiction writing.

Both Orwell's knee-jerk hostility toward abortion and his casual belief in men's sexual prerogatives reflect an unwillingness on the author's part to engage critically with feminist arguments about the political importance of women's bodily autonomy in the campaign for gender equality. In *Nineteen Eighty-Four*, Orwell represents Winston Smith's young lover, Julia, as the catalyst who spurs him toward political rebellion, but then has Winston dismiss Julia as only "a rebel from the waist down." But Julia arguably recognized what Winston failed to see, that the denial of a woman's bodily autonomy was as violent a tool of state control as censorship or thought policing. It was a message that Orwell never took to heart, and one that still divides twenty-first-century progressives, as we can see in the discomfort of many on the left as well as the right of the political spectrum with the #MeToo movement's demands for accountability and change to a culture of male sexual predation. The struggle of some otherwise progressive men to support that movement is strongly reminiscent of Orwell's own tortured fixation on abortion, which was colored by a conviction that male prerogatives should weigh as much if not more heavily than women's interests in questions of sexuality and reproduction.

ABORTION WAS DECRIMINALIZED IN BRITAIN IN 1967, WHEN PARliament made it legal to obtain an abortion before fetal viability, provided that the pregnant woman had the consent of two qualified doctors. Six years later, the US Supreme Court legalized abortion, stating in the majority opinion in *Roe v. Wade* that "the Due Process Clause of the Fourteenth Amendment . . . protects against state action the right to privacy, including a woman's qualified right to terminate her pregnancy." The *Roe* decision remained the law of the land in the United States for nearly fifty years, before being overturned on June 24, 2022, by the Supreme Court ruling *Dobbs v. Jackson Women's Health Organization*.

The ruling, which gives states the ability to decide on abortion's legality, has been denounced by feminists, who have characterized it as a blow to women's autonomy. The American family planning organization Planned Parenthood classifies the right to abortion as "the right to control your own body." It points to history to underscore the importance of legal abortion access, noting that, when abortion was criminalized, "providers and patients were pushed into the shadows," with serious consequences for women's social, emotional, and physical well-being.

Leaders on the political left have similarly railed against the decision. President Joe Biden characterized *Roe* as having been based on "basic principles of equality—that women have the power to control their own destiny. And it reinforced the fundamental right of privacy—the right of each of us to choose how to live our lives." Biden denounced the Supreme Court for taking the country backward by repealing an established right and vowed to do everything in his (limited) executive power to mitigate the impact of the decision on the American people.

As the historian Stephen Brooke has noted, support for Britain's Abortion Law Reform Association in the 1930s was principally drawn from the ranks of the Labour and Cooperative movement, which understood abortion access as not only a feminist but also a class issue. (Modern proponents of abortion rights have similarly noted that the criminalization of abortion disproportionately impacts poorer Black and minority ethnic women.) However, the leadership of interwar Labour never coalesced around abortion as a political issue. Some interwar progressives supported women's reproductive rights. Others, including Orwell, did not.

In 1936, Orwell wrote a novel about abortion—or at least, a novel in which an unplanned pregnancy and the decision not to have an abortion is the central climactic event which drives the story toward its inevitable denouement. In *Keep the Aspidistra Flying*, Orwell uses his semi-autobiographical antihero Gordon Comstock to articulate the view that abortion is beyond the pale, unjustifiable regardless of how this stance might jeopardize the possibility of liberation from capitalist toil. Revisiting the debate around abortion in the novel offers a valuable insight into the ongoing tensions over reproductive rights in our modern moment.

ORWELL'S NOVELS NEVER END HAPPILY EVER AFTER. THE PRE-dominantly male protagonists suffer invariably tragic fates. If women are not to blame for these tragedies per se, they are central to the men's undoing. In *Burmese Days*, John Flory takes his own life after being rejected by the fickle and self-serving woman on whom he had unwisely pinned his hopes of redemption from a life of physical and spiritual loneliness. In *Coming Up for Air*, George Bowling's great tragedy is that he hitched his wagon to the dour and domineering Hilda, a penny-pinching social climber who has condemned him to a life of suffocating suburban conformity. In *Nineteen Eighty-Four*, Winston Smith is inspired to his ultimately fatal acts of resistance by Julia, his beautiful, nymphomaniacal colleague at the Ministry of Truth, although he remains dismissive of her political acumen. Even in *Animal Farm*, it's the female show pony Molly who betrays her comrades by fraternizing with the neighboring farmers in exchange for pretty ribbons. But in none of Orwell's novels is the man's tragedy so clearly linked to a woman as in *Keep the Aspidistra Flying*.

A common houseplant, the eponymous aspidistra was a regular feature of interwar suburban sitting rooms, kitchen window-sills, and covered entries, as indeed it remains today. For most,

aspidistras, in their ubiquity and anonymity, barely even registered. But for Gordon, Orwell's soi-disant rebel against middle-
class respectability, the aspidistra in his rented lodgings becomes
a hated synecdoche for the entirety of middle-class life:

> Gordon had a sort of secret feud with the aspidistra. Many
> a time he had furtively attempted to kill it—starving it of
> water, grinding hot cigarette-ends against its stem, even
> mixing salt with its earth. But the beastly things are practi-
> cally immortal. In almost any circumstances they can pre-
> serve a wilting, diseased existence.

Try as he might, Gordon cannot kill the aspidistra, just as he cannot escape the bonds of "respectability" to which his class background, education, and morality condemn him. Early in the novel,
he expresses his determination not to "worship the money-god! To
settle down, to Make Good, to sell your soul for a villa and an
aspidistra!" By the book's final page, he has committed himself
to doing just that.

Gordon tries his best to avoid his fate. He quits his well-paying
job writing copy for an advertising agency and takes a minimum-
wage position as a bookseller, saving his intellectual energies to
devote to working on a book of poetry he seems destined never
to complete. (Orwell, too, worked in a London bookshop by day,
while writing in the evenings.) In Gordon's self-conception, he's
living a grim, but arguably noble, existence, until it is thrown into
chaos by—of course—a woman: "Rosemary, his girl, who loved
him—adored him, so she said—and who, all the same, had never
slept with him."

He spends most of the novel conniving to get Rosemary into

bed. He finally succeeds in convincing her, on a weekend holiday outside Slough, but she interrupts the act seconds before penetration when she realizes that he has not thought to bring contraception. The two lovers descend into a sordid squabble over why Rosemary can't just "take your chance," before sulking back to London in near silence. A few weeks later Rosemary, driven by love and pity for Gordon, agrees to go to bed with him. Their single, mutually unsatisfying sexual encounter results in Rosemary's becoming pregnant.

Shortly after their failed dalliance, Gordon and Rosemary have a falling-out. But then, three months later, she reappears on the scene, pregnant. Gordon does not take Rosemary's news well: "We shall have to get married, I suppose," he says flatly. Rosemary arguably stands to lose a lot more from this marriage than Gordon. After all, she has a stable job, and he is an underemployed deadbeat with a chip on his shoulder and delusions of being a poet. She's a decent person who genuinely loves him. He is a self-absorbed jerk.

In fact, he is such a self-absorbed jerk that Rosemary has assumed he would not want to marry her and has already looked into alternative arrangements. Rosemary doesn't want to be pregnant. In fact, she has already attempted to induce an abortion. As she says to Gordon: "It's been weeks now. If you knew the time I've had! I kept hoping and hoping—I took some pills—oh, it was too beastly!" (The "pills" Rosemary refers to were likely Beecham's pills or Penny Royal Bitter Apple, two common abortifacients that would have been familiar to 1930s readers.)

When the pills didn't work, she got a name of an abortionist from a colleague at work. As she tells Gordon, her colleague's friend had "had it done for only five pounds."

At this, the two look at one another.

"No fear!" he said. "Whatever happens we're not going to do *that*. It's disgusting."

"I know it is. But I can't have the baby without being married."

"No! If that's the alternative, I'll marry you. I'd sooner cut my right hand off than do a thing like that." . . .

He thought it over a little while longer. "It comes down to this. Either I marry you and go back to [my old advertising job], or you go to one of those filthy doctors and get yourself messed about for five pounds."

At this she twisted herself out of his grasp and stood up facing him. His blunt words had upset her. They had made the issue clearer and uglier than before.

"Oh, why did you say that?"

"Well, those *are* the alternatives."

It's a heartbreaking scene, particularly for Rosemary, although Orwell keeps the narrator's attention on Gordon. He is torn between holding on to his increasingly disappointing dream of living a life of poetic squalor or marrying a woman he doesn't love and raising their child in stultifying suburbia, a slave to the money god. Those aren't great options, but Rosemary's are worse. She either marries Gordon, who doesn't love her and would resent the marriage; has an illegal backroom abortion, with all of the attendant risk to both her womb and her life; or carries the baby to term on her own, is fired from her job for becoming pregnant, forced to rely on her family for financial support, and invites censure and social opprobrium.

The health risks of backroom abortions were—and remain—considerable. A 1937 UK government report on maternal mortality noted that abortions were both common and a common cause of puerperal mortality, leading to an estimated fourteen percent of maternal deaths. A 2009 article in the *Journal of Obstetrics and Gynaecology Canada* highlighted the continued risk of backstreet abortion, despite the development of antibiotics to treat sepsis. Abortions continue to account for more than a tenth of maternal deaths worldwide, and a quarter of women who resort to unsafe abortions suffer long-term health complications. An awareness of these risks helped to spur the formation of the Abortion Law Reform Association, a feminist pressure group founded in Britain in 1937 with the aim of legalizing abortion. (The national movement for abortion law reform in the United States did not emerge until after the Second World War, with Planned Parenthood organizing a national conference on abortion legalization in 1955, followed by the foundation of the National Association to Repeal Abortion Laws in 1969.)

While interwar British feminists sought to legalize abortion to protect the health of pregnant women, they also saw abortion access as an issue of equal rights. As Stella Browne wrote in 1935, "Abortion must be the key to a new world for women. . . . [F]reedom of choice and deliberate intention are necessary for women in their sexual relations and their maternity, if they are to make anything of their status and opportunities."

Browne's belief that abortion access was fundamentally a civil rights issue was later held by many second-wave feminists, including the US Supreme Court justice Ruth Bader Ginsburg, who long argued that the *Roe v. Wade* decision would have been on stronger footing had it grounded itself in a legal argument about women's equal rights as citizens, as opposed to an argument about women's right to privacy. In recent years, conserva-

tive anti-abortion activists have sought to turn Ginsburg's logic on
its head, arguing that modern anti-discrimination legislation and
maternity protections, as well as access to adoption, mean that
carrying a pregnancy to term no longer affects a woman's status
and opportunities.

Stella Browne proclaimed herself "a Socialist and 'extreme'
Left-Wing feminist," and several of her male socialist colleagues
did support her views on abortion access. Orwell's protagonist
Gordon Comstock, who is an anti-capitalist but skeptical of organized socialism, condemns socialists in part for their association
with abortion, telling his friend Ravelstein that, if actually implemented, socialism would probably look like "some kind of Aldous
Huxley *Brave New World*: only not so amusing. Four hours a day in
a model factory, tightening up bolt number 6003. Rations served
out in grease-proof paper at the communal kitchen. Community-
hikes from Marx Hostel to Lenin Hostel and back. Free abortion-
clinics on all the corners."

As with Orwell's quip about feminists and other cranks, here
was damnation by association. That said, whether you perceived
it in a positive or a negative light, the association between abortion rights and socialism only ran so deep. The Soviet Union
had legalized abortion in 1920, but it banned the procedure
again in 1936, the year in which *Keep the Aspidistra Flying* was
published, ostensibly due to concerns about medical risks, but
largely to combat population decline. The Soviets were supportive of a woman's right to choose only so long as her choice did
not imperil the strength of the state. While Social Democratic
administrations in Sweden and Denmark passed legislation
permitting abortion in limited circumstances in the late 1930s,
abortion remained illegal in most of Europe as well as in Britain

and the United States throughout Orwell's lifetime, despite the election of Labour and Social Democratic governments in several European countries.

Orwell's aversion to the procedure was grounded in a secular humanism that venerated the value and potential of all human life which made him, like many others across the political spectrum, hostile to abortion. He has Gordon struggle with the weight of the decision before him by going to the library and requesting two books on obstetrics. Leafing through the pages, he comes upon a sketch of a fetus at nine weeks:

> It gave him a shock to see it, for he had not expected it to look in the least like that. It was a deformed, gnomelike thing, a sort of clumsy caricature of a human being, with a huge domed head as big as the rest of its body. In the middle of the great blank expanse of head there was a tiny button of an ear. . . . It was a monstrous thing, and yet strangely human. It surprised him that they should begin looking human so soon. He had pictured something much more rudimentary; a mere blob of nucleus, like a bubble of frog-spawn.

It is this image that decides Gordon.

> His baby had seemed real to him from the moment when Rosemary spoke of abortion; but it had been a reality without visual shape—something that happened in the dark and was only important after it had happened. But here was the actual process taking place. Here was the poor ugly thing, no bigger than a gooseberry, that he had created by his heedless act. Its future, its continued existence perhaps, depended on

him. Besides, it was a bit of himself—it *was* himself. Dare
one dodge such a responsibility as that?

Gordon leaves the library and phones Rosemary. His mind is
made up. He will marry her.

The passage could have been written by a representative of Life,
the British anti-abortion organization that in 1990 sent models of
fetuses to MPs in an attempt to sway their votes on the Human Fer-
tilisation and Embryology Act, or by the authors of the legislation
on the books in several US states requiring women to undergo an
ultrasound and be presented with an image of their unborn fetus
before consenting to an abortion. The proliferation of ultrasound
technology in the 1970s changed the world's visual understanding
of pregnancy and helped fuel arguments about fetal personhood.
However, even before the advent of ultrasound, abortion opponents relied on emotive imagery to assert fetal humanity.

In the months before the decision to overturn *Roe v. Wade*,
two activists associated with the anti-abortion Family Research
Council wrote a piece in *Newsweek* magazine headlined "Abortion Advocates Are Resorting to Orwellian Language Games,"
which argued that pro-choice doctors were employing "Orwellian
techniques of linguistic manipulation by using antiseptic, medical language to mask the truth about abortion as murder." While
they appeared completely unaware of Orwell's own views on the
issue, they could have pointed out that the author himself was an
abortion opponent.

As pro-choice advocates within the United States and beyond
grapple with how to protect abortion rights in a post-*Roe* landscape, they could benefit from coming to terms with the extent
and origins of opposition to abortion within the progressive

coalition. Orwell scholars have routinely noted that, while a self-professed socialist, Orwell was a cultural conservative. Several have gone so far as to call him a "Tory radical" (akin to his sister Avril's description of him as a "Tory anarchist"). His views on reproductive politics offer a window into the lack of support for the birth control movement from many on the progressive left in the 1930s, even as most of those who did advocate for reproductive rights identified with the political left.

We can see echoes of Orwell's disquiet with campaigns for reproductive freedom in the hesitancy of many politicians on the left to fully embrace pro-choice politics today. For every Democratic leader like Pennsylvania senator John Fetterman, who flaunts his own pro-choice bona fides and has called out lukewarm supporters within his party with the admonition that, "if you are not willing to do whatever it takes to protect abortion rights when they are on the line, then you cannot call yourself pro-choice," there is a politician like Biden, who is less instinctively at ease leading America's pro-choice party. While Biden has since changed his tune on abortion rights, his staunch Catholicism had long left him out of step with much of his party on abortion. As a member of the Senate Judiciary Committee in 1982, he voted in committee in favor of a bill to amend the Constitution to allow states to outlaw abortion. He long opposed federal funding for abortions, only changing his position after launching his bid for the presidency in 2019, and, although his administration has since come out as a defender of a woman's right to choose, he has had comparatively little to say on the issue, a reticence that drew fire from feminists when he devoted only glancing attention to abortion politics in his first State of the Union address following the repeal of *Roe v. Wade*.

As with Biden, some Catholic members of the British Labour Party have taken a hard line on abortion rights. In 2008, Parliament held several unsuccessful votes to shorten the period during which a woman could receive an abortion on demand from twenty-four weeks. Fifteen percent of the Labour MPs who voted supported reducing the limit to twenty weeks. Seventeen Labour ministers voted to reduce the limit to twelve weeks, including Ruth Kelly, Des Brown, and Paul Murphy, who cited their Catholicism in justifying their vote, but not everyone who voted for the twelve-week limit was Catholic.

The Blair government had declared that Labour members would be given a "free vote" on the abortion limit. That is, Labour members were not whipped to vote for keeping the existing twenty-four-week ban in place. That decision reflects the long-standing uncertainty surrounding the place of feminism within left politics. The Labour Party has traditionally described itself as a broad church, and left parties across the West have similarly positioned themselves as inclusive of a wide range of progressive viewpoints. Yet, there has long been an implicit hierarchy behind that inclusivity, with the class struggle taking precedence over not only gender politics, but also frequently over issues of race, sexuality, and disability. One study of women in the post-WWII German revolutionary socialist movement described women's oppression tellingly as a "'secondary contradiction' produced by capitalism that would be resolved once the 'primary contradiction'—class differences—was eliminated." Orwell's writing offers an insight into how one male author, writing in the 1930s, could understand himself to be politically progressive, but reject feminists' arguments that women's reproductive autonomy was central to their equal participation in society and hence central to a progressive political agenda. Focusing on Orwell's gender politics offers a perspective on the long history of feminism's contested place under the umbrella of progressive politics. It is also a reminder that, while Orwell's writing offers enduring insights about the importance of liberty, the corruption of power, and the threat posed by inequality, he was not without his limitations and prejudices. While many interwar writers—male and female—did think critically about the mechanics of patriarchy and the place of women in their society, Orwell was not one of them.

ORWELL'S PROBLEMATIC ATTITUDE TOWARD ABORTION IS ULTImately much less troubling than the attitude toward sexual power that repeatedly recurs in his writing. Recent years have witnessed a fierce debate within the progressive camp over whether and when it is appropriate to "cancel" political allies on account of their sexual transgressions, particularly as many claim that the political right does not hold its own side to a similar ethical standard. In reading Orwell's writing and evaluating the evidence of his past, we need to ask ourselves not only how previous readers' unwillingness to take issue with Orwell's sexual politics both reflected and enabled a world in which male predation remains pervasive, but also whether we, as twenty-first-century readers, should hold Orwell in lower esteem because of his sexual politics.

LIKE MOST PEOPLE, MY FIRST EXPOSURE TO ORWELL'S WRITING about humans—as opposed to animals—was reading *Nineteen Eighty-Four*. In 1995, no one thought to issue trigger warnings for texts, like the one that the University of Northampton provocatively slapped on the novel in 2022, letting students know that the book addresses "challenging issues related to violence, gender, sexuality, class, race, abuses, sexual abuse, political ideas and offensive language." My male English teacher at my all-girls high school certainly did not have it in him to discuss the violence of Winston's sexual fantasies with a group of sixteen-year-olds. And so, it was without warning or mental preparation that I turned the page of my Signet Classic edition to read of Winston transferring his hate from the image of Emmanuel Goldstein depicted on Big Brother's telescreens to the body of Julia, "the dark-haired girl behind him," whose name he did not yet know.

> Vivid, beautiful hallucinations flashed through his mind. He would flog her to death with a rubber truncheon. He would tie her naked to a stake and shoot her full of arrows like Saint Sebastian. He would ravish her and cut her throat at the moment of climax. Better than before, moreover, he realized why it was that he hated her. He hated her because she was young and pretty and sexless, because he wanted to go to bed with her and would never do so, because round her sweet supple waist, which seemed to ask you to encircle it with your arm, there was only the odious scarlet sash, aggressive symbol of chastity.

Winston's violent desire to rape and murder Julia is relayed without comment and then quickly passed over, as Orwell returns to his description of Oceania's ritual "Two Minutes Hate." Several chapters later, however, Orwell reprises his theme. Julia, it turns out, is not as unobtainable as Winston had supposed. Despite the fact that he is thirty-nine years old, has "a wife that I can't get rid

of," varicose veins and "five false teeth," *she* seduces *him*. Winston
is so overcome with "incredulity and pride," that she has chosen
him that he decides to make her "a sort of love-offering," by honestly sharing with her his previous violent fantasies:

> "I hated the sight of you," he said. "I wanted to rape you
> and then murder you afterwards. Two weeks ago I thought
> seriously of smashing your head in with a cobblestone.
> I honestly thought you had something to do with the
> Thought Police."

Julia's response to this revelation, rather implausibly, is to "laug[h]
delightedly."

We never discussed either passage in my high school English
class, although we did get into Winston's chauvinistic dismissal
of Julia's rebellion as grounded in sexual liberation, not "political"
opposition. We were a progressive all-girls high school, after all.
Nonetheless, the brutality of Winston's fantasy lingered with me,
until it came back with a jolt when I picked up a copy of *Down
and Out in Paris and London* on a trip to Britain during my senior
year of college.

In the first half of *Down and Out*, Orwell offers a fictionalized account of his time living in Paris's Latin Quarter and
includes several vignettes of characters he meets there, including an exceptionally lengthy discussion of "Charlie, one of the
local curiosities," who liked to "discourse to you of love." One
evening, Charlie, "a youth of family and education who had
run away from home and lived on occasional remittances,"
decides to render "the true meaning of love—what is the true
sensibility, the higher, more refined pleasure which is known

to civilized men alone." What follows is a story of exceptional pornographic violence.

Charlie steals a thousand francs from his visiting brother and uses the money to bribe an old madam to let him have sex with a girl, who may or may not have been procured from the neighboring convent. He hands the madam the money, and, "'*Voilà!*' she said; 'go down into the cellar there and do what you like. I shall see nothing, hear nothing, know nothing. You are free, you understand—perfectly free.'"

Charlie makes full use of his freedom in a sadistic scene luridly described by Orwell, who purports to be quoting Charlie's own words:

> She gave a whimper of fright. With a bound I was beside the bed; she tried to elude me, but I seized her by the throat—like this, do you see?—tight! She struggled, she began to cry out for mercy, but I held her fast, forcing back her head and staring down into her face. She was twenty years old, perhaps; her face was the broad, dull face of a stupid child, but it was coated with paint and powder, and her blue, stupid eyes, shining in the red light, wore that shocked, distorted look that one sees nowhere save in the eyes of these women. She was some peasant girl, doubtless, whom her parents had sold into slavery.
>
> Without another word I pulled her off the bed and threw her on to the floor. And then I fell upon her like a tiger! . . . More and more savagely I renewed the attack. Again and again the girl tried to escape; she cried out for mercy anew, but I laughed at her.

"Mercy!" I said, "do you suppose I have come here to
show mercy? Do you suppose I have paid a thousand francs
for that?" I swear to you, *messieurs et dames*, that if it were
not for that accursed law that robs us of our liberty, I would
have murdered her at that moment.

Charlie's tale goes on for five excruciating pages of what is effectively snuff, until he ends with, "That is Love. That was the hap-
piest day of my life." Orwell's only comment on the scene that he
has just related is, "He was a curious specimen, Charlie. I describe
him, just to show what diverse characters could be found flourish-
ing in the Coq d'Or quarter."

Over the following years, I've searched for a contemporary book
review that drew attention to the gratuitous awfulness of the scene,
to no avail. The only contemporary mention of "Charlie" that I've
ever located is in a *Tribune* review of the book's wartime reissue,
wherein the reviewer writes, "The Parisians with whom the writer
associates are fascinating creatures. I can't get over Charlie. . . . As
his historian remarks, he was a curious specimen." No mention of
his depravity or sadism. The contemporary published reviews of
Down and Out that I have located are all by men, and hence we
have no record of how women viewed the Charlie scene at the time.
In fact, as Daphne Patai has written, we have little record of contemporary female readers' thoughts on any of Orwell's oeuvre.
"Where," she laments in *The Orwell Mystique*, "are the women readers of his works who heard and took seriously the misogyny of his
texts. . . . Perhaps they did not have access to the press, as did his
male readers; or their own perceptions tended to be diminished,
even stilled, by the roar of respect he seemed to generate."

In his 2022 book *Orwell and Empire,* Douglas Kerr includes a chapter entitled "Women" that deals head on with the extreme violence of *Down and Out*'s Charlie scene. Kerr suggests that the scene, in which the "wretched French girl . . . [i]nfantilized, brutalized, powerless, and silenced after crying out for mercy, exotically coated with paint and powder (like a Burmese girl wearing thanaka cream on her face), and essentialized ('these women'), . . . comes in the trappings of Orientalism," may have been intended as a veiled critique of "the structures of power in colonial Burma," of which it could be said to represent a "distilled version." Personally, in light of Orwell's other writing, I find it difficult to accept this special pleading. Yet, at the least, Kerr makes an effort to look directly at Orwell's literary sexual violence.

————

ONCE YOU START TO LOOK FOR SIGNS OF MISOGYNY AND SADISM in Orwell's writing, they become hard to escape. Not only are women often depicted as the objects—real or imagined—of sexual violence, but they are also repeatedly depicted in animalistic terms, as when "Charlie" describes his victim first as a "chicken" and later as a tiger's prey. In *Burmese Days*, the main character, Flory, has a Burmese concubine whom he "had bought . . . from her parents two years ago, for three hundred rupees." Flory treats Ma Hla May abominably. After one of their sexual encounters, he shouts at her, "Get out of this room! I told you to go. I don't want you in here after I've done with you." When she protests, "That is a nice way to speak to me! You treat me as though I were a prostitute," Flory retorts, "So you are. Out you go."

Given our knowledge of Orwell's anti-imperialism, it might initially seem credible that Orwell is using the character of Ma

Hla May to critique gender relations in colonial Burma—that the
reader is intended to sympathize with Ma Hla May and condemn
Flory. But such a reading is undermined by other passages in the
book, in which the narrator gratuitously describes the young
woman in language that is incompatible with any feminist reading of his writing. He describes her, variously, as having "rather
nice teeth, like the teeth of a kitten," "passive yet pleased and
faintly smiling, like a cat which allows one to stroke it," and as a
creature who "crept, wormlike, right across the floor to his feet." If
Orwell wrote the relationship between Flory and Ma Hla May to
express imperial guilt or reveal imperial inhumanity, then why is
the dehumanized figure not her white colonial "master"?

In *Keep the Aspidistra Flying*, Gordon laments that humans
cannot "at least be like the animals—minutes of ferocious lust and
months of icy chastity. Take a cock pheasant, for example. He jumps
up on the hens' backs without so much as a with your leave or by
your leave. And no sooner is it over than the whole subject is out
of his mind. He hardly even notices his hens any longer; he ignores
them, or simply pecks them if they come too near his food."

And in the original draft of *A Clergyman's Daughter*, Orwell
had explained the titular heroine's sudden amnesia and descent
into the London underworld as driven by a dissociative episode
after the local rogue Mr. Warburton "tried to rape Dorothy." After
having allowed the "Charlie" scene to appear in *Down and Out*,
Orwell's publisher, Victor Gollancz, here insisted that Orwell tone
down his prose, at the advice of his lawyer, so that the published
version ultimately ran:

> But at the same moment Mr Warburton, invisible behind
> her chair, had lowered his hands and taken her gently by

the shoulders. Dorothy immediately wriggled herself in an effort to get free of him; but Mr Warburton pressed her back into her place.

"Keep still," he said peaceably.

"Let me go!" exclaimed Dorothy. . . .

"But I don't particularly want to let you go," objected Mr Warburton.

"PLEASE don't stroke my arm like that! I don't like it!"

"What a curious child you are! Why don't you like it?"

"I tell you I don't like it!"

At that point, Dorothy jumps up from her chair and prepares to flee the house, while Mr. Warburton faces her "entirely unconcerned" and "totally devoid of shame." In the rewriting, Warburton is transformed from a rapist to a lecher. Given Gollancz's willingness to publish the Charlie scene in *Down and Out*, one has to assume that it was not squeamishness about the fact of rape that led him to request the change. It may well have been the combination of the rape scene with Orwell's presentation of Dorothy as a frigid prude who has an abnormal aversion to "ALL THAT!" (a.k.a. sex) and is so repressed that she expiates sinful thoughts by pricking her wrist with a straight pin, whereas Warburton is depicted as an outlandish, but largely harmless, middle-aged cad. Had Gollancz allowed the rape scene to stand, one suspects that some of his readers might have found the novel's undertone of victim-blaming difficult to stomach, even in the comparatively misogynistic 1930s.

In *Coming Up for Air*, the protagonist, George Bowling, doesn't fantasize about raping his wife, but he does think about murdering her: "Of course in practice one never does these things, they're only a kind of fantasy that one enjoys thinking about. Besides, chaps who murder their wives always get copped. . . . After a year or two I stopped wanting to kill her and started wondering about her." Orwell clearly thought the passage a joke, and it was apparently a brand of humor that he fortunately shared with his first wife, Eileen. (Five months into her marriage, Eileen wrote to a friend, "During the first few weeks of marriage . . . we quarrelled so continuously & really bitterly that I thought I'd save time & just write to everyone when the murder or separation had been accomplished.") Yet, given the prevalence of gendered violence in Orwell's writing, it's a joke in poor taste. In the same novel, Bowling recalls his first girlfriend, Elsie, with fond approbation, as "very submissive. . . . As soon as you saw her you knew that you could take her in your arms and do what you wanted with her."

Orwell's views on reproductive rights, his demeaning manner in writing about women, and his seeming casual acceptance of sexual violence cannot simply be dismissed as products of their time. As discussed above, there were feminist voices in the 1930s and 1940s arguing for greater reproductive freedoms for women and making a broader case for women's equality in personal, professional, and political spheres. Feminist authors addressed these themes in literature, as in the 1929 novel *Clash* by Ellen Wilkinson, which depicts a group of working-class women candidly discussing what a lack of reproductive autonomy means to themselves and their families and complaining that Catholic politicians within the Labour movement ignore the harms that prohibitions on family planning pose to women. Or, in Winifred Holtby's *South Riding* (1936), in which an intelligent and ambitious school mistress struggles with her own sexual and political identity, while at the same time seeking to ensure that a favored pupil from a working-class community does not miss out on the opportunity to realize her potential because of her obligations to care for her family. Or the American author Djuna Barnes's *Nightwood* (1936), in which the heroine comes to terms with both her dissatisfaction with marriage and motherhood and her same-sex attraction, and ultimately embraces nonconformity with societal expectations through literal transformation. Or, of course, Zora Neale Hurston's *Their Eyes Were Watching God* (1937), which offers a sensitive, intersectional look at gender and race in the early twentieth century in a way that *Burmese Days* signally fails to do.

While nearly all feminist fiction at this time was written by female authors, such works were consumed and discussed by male as well as female readers—although notably not by Orwell. Each of the four novels mentioned above was reviewed in the *Times Literary Supplement*. Three of the titles were reviewed by men. Male authors reviewed *Nightwood* and *Their Eyes Were Watching God* in the *New York Times*. Orwell himself was a prodigious reviewer of both fiction and nonfiction throughout his career. The four-volume *Collected Essays, Journalism and Letters of George Orwell* contains sixty-four of his published book reviews. Only two of these are books sole-authored by women. (Another two are jointly authored books on the Spanish War with a female contributor.) It was not that feminist literature—or, for that matter, literature by female writers—did not exist in Orwell's time; rather, he failed to engage with it, let alone take its arguments seriously.

———

FOR THE MOST PART, ORWELL SEEMS TO HAVE BEEN LET OFF THE hook about his gender politics by his contemporary reviewers, who notably were almost exclusively male. To the extent that we have a sense of how contemporary women viewed Orwell, it comes from his correspondence with his female friends, many of whom were his former girlfriends or would-be girlfriends. In July 1934, Orwell wrote to Brenda Salkeld (who had years before turned down his marriage proposal), relaying a luncheon with a feminist friend. In what Orwell appears to have intended as teasing flirtation, he wrote Salkeld that his friend "tells me that my anti-feminist views are probably due to Sadism! I have never read the Marquis de Sade's novels—they are unfortunately very hard to get hold of" (a reference to the books' censorship in Britain). Later, Salkeld, speaking on a BBC program in 1960, said curtly of Orwell, "He didn't really like women." Her sense that Orwell was at heart a misogynist was likely to have been fueled by a letter he sent her after marrying first wife Eileen O'Shaughnessy in 1936. In it, he revealed that he had discussed his continued attraction to Brenda with Eileen and that she "wished I could sleep with you abt [about] twice a year, just to keep me happy." Orwell presumably intended this to be flattering or flirtatious—if not a serious overture. Most women would read it as profoundly disrespectful to both his wife and would-be mistress.

But a sense of disquiet is only magnified when we take into account that Orwell may have been not only a chronicler, but a practitioner of sexual predation in his day. In 2006, Dione Venables, the poet Jacintha Buddicom's cousin, wrote a postscript for a reissue of Buddicom's memoir *Eric & Us*, a portrait of her and her brother Prosper's childhood living next door to the Blairs in the village of Shiplake. According to Venables, an eighteen-year-old Eric Blair sexually assaulted then twenty-year-old Buddicom in 1921. The revelations came out before the onset of the #MeToo movement and elicited comparatively little comment from Orwell scholars at the time. In the postscript, Venables claimed that, in a letter from her cousin to Eric, written long ago and since destroyed, she had recalled the details of Eric's assault on her shortly before he returned to Eton for his final term. Venables had only heard of the letter's contents secondhand, but in her retelling, "During the course of one of their almost daily walks . . . Eric, it seems, had attempted to take things further and make SERIOUS love to Jacintha. He had held her down (by that time he was 6'4" and she was still under 5') and though she struggled, yelling at him to STOP, he had torn her skirt and badly bruised a shoulder and her left hip." The episode put an end to their adolescent friendship.

Venables' relation of the incident speaks both to its importance in the minds of Buddicom's immediate family and to the sexual politics of her generation. Venables, who was seventy when she published the postscript in 2006, includes a caveat that Jacintha "*must* have realized that Eric was not entirely to blame over this incident because she had not stopped his adolescent romancing earlier."

Few who have come of age after the 1960s would publicly contend that Jacintha had had it coming to her for leading Eric Blair on—although many might continue to sympathize quietly with that interpretation. The lack of rethinking of Orwell's character and legacy immediately following the *Eric & Us* reissue reveals the limits of social and cultural change over the intervening decades. At that point, with the Cold War seemingly consigned to the dustbin of history, Orwell's torch was largely carried by those on the political left, which in the United States was still grappling with the impact of Bill Clinton's impeachment and the contortions to which many Democrats had submitted themselves to defend the former president's predatory sexual behaviors for the sake of preserving a tenuous Democratic hold on Washington.

In Britain, Orwell biographer Gordon Bowker owned up to the likely veracity of Venables' tale in a 2007 piece in the *Times Literary Supplement*. I think it's worth bringing up his critique of it again. He casually refers to the assault as "a rape," before downgrading it in his concluding observation that "the countryside ramble leading to the sudden [now] pounce does not just feature in his fiction, it was his preferred mode of seduction." (Bowker's article was provocatively titled "Blair Pounces"—a play on Orwell's given name and the name of the then prime minister, Tony Blair, who for all his other sins was decidedly not, unlike his American Democrat counterpart, a "pouncer.") Female readers were similarly disinclined to make too much of the revelations, with the author Kathryn Hughes writing in the *Guardian* that "the attempted 'rape' . . . in truth, sounds more like a botched seduction."

In the light of our current understanding of sexual harassment and assault, Orwell's casual disregard for women's bodily autonomy—in both his writing and, apparently, in his youthful practice—have become harder to ignore. Thus, John Sutherland's *Orwell's Nose*, published in 2018, deals squarely with his attack on Jacintha, with Sutherland terming it an "act of crass inexperience, on Eric's part," but nonetheless an "assault" and one that might well have ended with him "fac[ing] Wandsworth Prison rather than Rangoon." Whereas in D. J. Taylor's 2003 *Orwell: The Life*, the only assaults are military, his updated 2023 biography, *Orwell: The New Life*, includes discussions of Orwell's sexual "assaults" on Buddicom, Salkeld, and Eileen Blair's university friend Lydia

Jackson. And Anna Funder's *Wifedom: Mrs. Orwell's Invisible Life*
puts Orwell's sexual transgressions at the forefront of her retelling
of the Orwell marriage.

The question that we are left with is how, or even whether, a
consideration of Orwell's sexual behavior and the assumed power
dynamics that underlie it should impact our appreciation of the
man and the author. In previous chapters, we have talked about
modern "cancel culture" in the sense of the "cancellation" or informal censorship of ideas by groups on either the left or right of the
political spectrum. However, "cancel culture" has another connotation to do with the "cancellation" of previously respected or venerated individuals because of revelations about their attitudes or
actions that arguably delegitimize their claims to our respect. This
second definition is most frequently used by those on the political right, who cry foul at the supposed cancellation of (almost
invariably) old or dead white men by the alleged "wokeratti,"
when progressive voices are most often asking, not for a *Nineteen
Eighty-Four*-style erasure of the past, but a more nuanced discussion of the intersections between individuals' personal lives and
their creative or political personas.

In 2018, the *Daily Mail* columnist Craig Brown wrote a piece
tracing a litany of Orwell's "dirty old man" perversions, from his
frequenting of prostitutes—including after he and Eileen were
married—to his repeated unwelcome advances on women, to his
alleged assault of Buddicom, and he noted that, "[i]n the current
climate, Orwell might even find himself in court on a charge
of historic sex abuse." He ended his column by asking rhetori-
cally, "Does this mean the works of George Orwell should be
removed from libraries and bookshops?" to which he replied,
"Of course not. But if he is to be excused, then why not other

literary heroes?" It is a difficult question—not least because it is near impossible to come up with any literary heroes whose works have been removed from libraries or bookshops because of their personal sexual conduct. (The closest analogy might be, not with authors, but with directors, as both Roman Polanski and Woody Allen have faced significant, albeit informal, censure for their alleged sexual misconduct.)

Does the recognition that his sexual attitudes were loathsome mean that one should no longer engage seriously with his defense of freedom or his critique of authoritarianism? There are those who would doubtless say yes, just as there are those who would discount Thomas Jefferson's writings on liberty because their author enslaved people and sexually exploited and fathered children by Sally Hemings, an enslaved woman. But, "canceling" Orwell—or anyone, for that matter—risks throwing the baby out with the bathwater. There is still much that is prescient and valuable in Orwell's writing, both for understanding his own era and for making sense of our own. Further, by continuing to engage with Orwell's writing in its entirety—including its discomforting depictions of sexual predation—we can gain a clearer understanding of the long, embedded history of sexual harassment and predatory behavior even among those who believe themselves to be enlightened and on the right side of history. And, hopefully, a clearer understanding of that history can help cement a path toward future change.

Finally, a clear appreciation of Orwell's gender politics helps us to approach his constructive proposals for social democratic reform with a clear eye, and to appreciate both the extent and the limitations of the reforms he proposed. While Orwell was astute about the need for revolutionary change to Britain's class structure and to its imperial relations, he remained broadly uninterested in issues affecting women or related to gender relations. The inter-sections between class and gender in shaping British social life remained unexplored in Orwell's writing, with the consequence that Orwell's proposals appear both radical and limited from the perspective of the twenty-first century.

6

BLUEPRINT FOR REVOLUTION

Making the Case for Democratic Socialism

George Orwell was, first and foremost, a social critic. He was much better at identifying the problems with capitalism, imperialism, communism, and fascism than he was at generating concrete proposals for how to create a more just and equal society. He would not have made a great civil servant, nor fellow at a policy think tank. In his 1946 essay "Why I Write," he contended, "Every line of serious work that I have written since 1936 has been written, directly or indirectly, *against* totalitarianism and *for* democratic socialism, as I understand it." The first half of his assertion is demonstrably true. The second half is more debatable.

While Orwell rarely offered constructive solutions, neither did he stand silently by. Rather, he took a frequently controversial and unpopular stand against injustice. He succumbed neither to the cynicism that prevents Benjamin the donkey in *Animal Farm* from speaking out against the revolution until it is too late, nor the political quietism that he tendentiously claimed to admire in his 1940 essay "Inside the Whale." Yet, the criticism that Victor Gollancz levied against him in a preface to *The Road to Wigan Pier* stands: "Mr. Orwell does not once define what he means by Socialism; nor does he explain how the oppressors oppress, nor even what he understands by the words 'liberty' and 'justice.'" Gollancz viewed Part II of the book, in which Orwell outlines what he perceived to be the failures of the British socialist movement, as a damp squib, in that it didn't address the "great deal of hard work and hard thinking to be done—less noble and more humdrum than the appeal to generosities, but no less important if a real victory is to be won" in the war against inequality.

The one place where Orwell did clearly articulate the case *for* democratic socialism was in *The Lion and the Unicorn: Socialism and the English Genius*, the brief book that he wrote during the Blitz of 1940–41. Along with a few other World War II essays, we'll see that it represents Orwell's most concrete attempt to draft a blueprint for a truly English revolution—how the country he loved could throw off the capitalist-imperialist yoke that he hated and build a social democratic future. Orwell saw the war as a moment that had "turned Socialism from a text-book word into a realizable policy." "The inefficiency of private capitalism has been proved all over Europe. Its injustice has been proved in the East End of London," he wrote. By exposing the bankruptcy of capitalism, the war had for the first time made socialism "both revolutionary and realistic."

In fact, Orwell argued that the circumstances of the war had made a socialist revolution not only possible, but necessary. The total mobilization of society that the war demanded could not be achieved without revolutionizing the command and control of the economy, and the shared sacrifice that the war effort required could not be sustained unless equality of sacrifice were met with true equality of opportunity, both within the British Isles and for the nations Britain had colonized overseas.

SHOULD WE SEE ORWELL AS NAIVE SINCE A GENUINE SOCIALIST revolution never came about? Certainly, by the time of his death, Orwell had come to see his earlier hopes for the future as naive, as much as he supported the comparatively moderate reforms of the postwar Labour government. To truly understand his politics, Orwell biographer Peter Stansky proposes in *The Socialist Patriot: George Orwell and War*, one needs to delve into Orwell's simultaneous commitment to social revolution and his love for the soul and traditions of England. In Stansky's analysis, Orwell was an uneasy admixture of those two eighteenth-century luminaries Edmund Burke, the great Whig statesman, and Thomas Paine, the tribune of the rights of man. This duality is what allowed Orwell "[t]o be loyal both to Chamberlain's England and to the England of tomorrow," or what allowed him, as his first wife, Eileen, caustically put it, "to be a Socialist though Tory."

But what did Orwell imagine the "England of tomorrow" to be? How would it differ from, and how would it continue to remain essentially, the England of today?

FIRST AND FOREMOST, THE ENGLAND OF TOMORROW WOULD BE more socially and economically equal. In chapter 4, we discussed how Orwell's early writing put almost as much emphasis on the abolition of the class system as it did on the reduction in income

inequality. The social component of equality was again emphasized in *Homage to Catalonia*, where he praised revolutionary
Barcelona for its seeming abolition of class hierarchies, even as
the social transformation unnerved him. ("everyone called everyone else 'Comrade' and 'Thou,' and said 'Salud!' instead of 'Buenos
dias'. . . . The wealthy classes had practically ceased to exist. . . . All
this was queer and moving. There was much in it that I did not
understand, in some ways I did not even like it, but I recognized
it immediately as a state of affairs worth fighting for.")

But, the experience of war in Britain brought to the fore the
material significance of economic difference, and what it meant
to ask for equality of sacrifice in a world where people have such
different access to resources. Thus, in April 1940, even before the
evacuation of Dunkirk and the start of the Blitz, Orwell wrote to
a friend that it was "vitally necessary to do something towards
equalizing incomes" if the war were to be won. In *The Lion and
the Unicorn*, Orwell proposed, as a practical step toward social
revolution, "limitation of incomes" such that "the highest tax-free
income in Britain does not exceed the lowest by more than ten
to one." As implied by the word *limitation*, income gaps would
be reduced principally, not by dramatically raising the salaries of
manual and clerical workers, but by taxing the unearned wealth of
those at the top of the income ladder and redistributing the pro-
ceeds to society's worse off through tax relief and welfare spending. In the same work, Orwell insisted that "the underlying fact
was that the whole position of the moneyed class had long ceased
to be justifiable. . . . They were simply parasites, less useful to society than his fleas are to a dog."

When Orwell was writing in 1940, the expropriation of the
wealth of Britain's financial elite could, practically, have come

about in only a handful of ways: through the imposition of a one-time wealth tax or an ongoing progressive income and capital gains tax; through the democratic passage of legislation to nationalize major industries and financial services without financial compensation for private stockholders; or through the revolutionary seizure of the wealthy's capital assets. Orwell was clear that the nation's major capital assets should be nationalized—an inconvenient opinion for those who would claim him for the political right. In addition to the limitation of incomes, his program for an English revolution includes "nationalization of land, mines, railways, banks and major industries." Yet, he does not expand on how this nationalization should occur. At the time he wrote, excepting the temporary wartime nationalization of major industries by the British government during both the First and Second World Wars, and a similar scheme in France in the late 1930s, the principal model of nationalization was the Soviet Union, where state control had been achieved at the point of the sword.

Orwell also asserted that violence might be necessary to achieve the type of social revolution he envisaged. In "My Country Right or Left" (1940), he prophesized that, as the war continued, it would inevitably propel "changes that will surprise the idiots who have no foresight. I dare say the London gutters will have to run with blood. All right, let them, if it is necessary." And in 1941's "Socialism and Democracy," Orwell contended, "When the real English Socialist movement appears . . . it will cut across the existing party divisions. It will be both revolutionary and democratic." The potential for violence was implicit in his contention that "there is no strong reason for thinking that any really fundamental change can ever be achieved peacefully." But, despite his suggestion that violence, if necessary, was justifiable, there is no indication that

Orwell believed democratic socialism in England would neces-
sitate a bloody civil war.

On the contrary, much of his wartime writing exalted the British commitment to the rule of law. In *The Lion and the Unicorn*,
he identifies as "an all-important English trait . . . the respect for
constitutionalism and legality, the belief in 'the law' as something
above the State and above the individual, something which is cruel
and stupid, of course, but at any rate *incorruptible*."

So, was it possible to nationalize wealth and drastically reduce
income inequality constitutionally and democratically? The
answer proved to be yes and no—or yes, to a limited extent.

THE POSTWAR PERIOD SAW THE IMPLEMENTATION OF MIXED
economies of state and private ownership across the Western
world. It was matched in the 1950s by an increase in progressive
taxation that saw top marginal income tax rates of over ninety
percent in the United States and the United Kingdom. Rising tax
rates, combined with an increase in redistributive spending on
social welfare programs, led to a drastic reduction of inequality,
with the Gini coefficient, a common statistical measure of societal
inequality, falling to historic lows across Europe and the United
States by the 1970s. In the US, the expansion of Social Security
in the 1950s and the introduction of Medicare and Medicaid a
decade later helped to protect millions of Americans from destitution and disease. In Britain, the implementation of the National
Health Service, universal pensions, and child allowances by the
postwar Attlee government drastically improved the lives of Britain's poorest. (These universal benefits disproportionately benefited women, who had previously been largely excluded from

Britain's limited welfare systems developed in the early twentieth century, a product of the patriarchal order Orwell consistently overlooked in his writing on inequality.)

Yet, in no Western country did equality approach the level proposed by Orwell, in part because the nationalization of major industries was principally achieved not through appropriation, but through the purchase of private shares by the state with compensation to the former owners—much as the abolition of slavery in the British Empire in 1833 had been accompanied by the payment of compensation to former slave owners such as Orwell's great-great-grandfather. The determination to compensate capitalists for the nationalization of industries in the 1940s owed much to the British ideas of the rule of law and "fair play" that Orwell championed. The postwar Labour government, despite the party's professed socialism, was almost as deeply committed to the inviolable rights of property as the capitalists themselves.

In his summer 1946 "London Letter" for the American publication *Partisan Review*, Orwell noted with chagrin Labour's determination to (over-) compensate the capitalist classes for the UK's rail service: "The railway shareholders are being bought out at prices they would hardly get in the open market: still, the control of the railways is being taken out of private hands," and hence, "I suppose, the drift is towards socialism." Those who had invested in transport and utility companies remained capitalists after nationalization; their wealth was still able to reap its "unearned increment," only now it did so principally by drawing interest on government debt or seeking investment opportunities in the global market. Higher tax rates reduced capital gains, but did not abolish them, and, as the economist Thomas Piketty has documented, the return on capital has grown faster than real wages since the Second World War, with the result that the rich have only gotten richer.

While no other Western country outside the Soviet bloc embraced nationalization with the fervor of the British Labour government, European countries similarly pursued a model of nationalizing major industries with generous compensation to shareholders. Only the US largely eschewed the rush toward a mixed economy that emerged after the Second World War. Unco-incidentally, the US also remained the most economically unequal NATO state. The share of income that went to the top ten percent of earners never fell below a third.

The Second World War had created a political opening for unprecedented economic redistribution, but the opening proved to be limited in both its size and its duration. It was not the per-manent economic revolution that Orwell had hoped to see. But his sense of hope that an opportunity had arisen for a seismic shift is one that resonates strongly with far more recent events. Orwell briefly believed that the "Spirit of the Blitz" could be harnessed to revolutionize society. Many commentators saw the COVID-19 pandemic as Britain's twenty-first-century Blitz, and hoped that the shared experience of tragedy and sacrifice would engender a new social revolution.

While scholars, including Jose Harris and Steven Fielding, have argued that any wartime change in social attitudes was both more superficial and more ephemeral than is commonly under-stood, the myth of the Blitz has persisted, albeit with less and less emphasis placed on its connection to the 1945 Labour victory. Indeed, Boris Johnson's Conservative government made consid-erable use of the analogy of the Blitz in its appeals to the British people during the early days of the COVID pandemic in 2020. To take one of many examples, Matt Hancock, then Britain's secretary of state for health, intoned, "Our generation has never been tested like this. Our grandparents were, during the Second World War. . . . Despite the pounding every night, the rationing, the loss of life, they pulled together in one gigantic national effort. Today our generation is facing its own test, fighting a very real and new disease." Such analogies were not only deployed by members of the government. The "Forces' sweetheart" of the war, Dame Vera Lynn, made the connection explicit, issuing a statement just before her 103rd birthday: "In these uncertain times, I am taken back to my time during World War Two, when we all pulled together and looked after each other. It is this spirit that we all need to find again to weather the storm of the coronavirus." And Prime Minister Boris Johnson extended the wartime metaphor from the fight against the virus ravaging the country to the fight against the ravaging of the British economy as a result of economic disruption: "We must act as in wartime and do everything it takes to support the economy."

While such comparisons were more common in the UK, the British did not corner the market on World War II analogies. In March 2020, US president Donald Trump reminded journalists of Americans' sacrifice during the Second World War and then announced, "Now it's our time. We must sacrifice together, because we are all in this together, and we will come through together." French president Emmanuel Macron used the language of war in his televised address announcing the implementation of lockdown restrictions on March 16, 2020. Even German chancellor Angela Merkel reached for the analogy, despite her own country's role in World War II. Two days after Macron, Merkel made a televised address to the German people, emphasizing that, "since

German unification, no, since the Second World War, there has
been no challenge to our nation that has demanded such a degree
of common and united action."

————————

GEORGE ORWELL WOULD HAVE SEEN MUCH THAT WAS FAMILIAR
in those early days of the COVID emergency, not only in the surge
of national unity that it engendered in countries across the globe,
but also in the way that it seemingly awakened both citizens and
governments to the reality that "the economic system by which
they lived was unjust, inefficient and out-of-date." All of a sudden, a broad consensus emerged both around the need for the
state to direct private enterprise to produce more personal protective equipment and to rapidly develop COVID vaccines, and
around the need, not only to support large corporations, but to
provide direct financial support for individuals hardest hit by
the global economic shutdown. The consensus spurred a raft of
"socialistic" legislation on both sides of the Atlantic. In the UK,
then Chancellor of the Exchequer Rishi Sunak's furlough policy
helped over eleven million workers pay their bills while businesses
shuttered during the worst days of the pandemic. In the United
States, extended and augmented unemployment benefits helped
to sustain those out of work as a consequence of COVID, whereas
COVID stimulus payments—in the form of paper checks that
Donald Trump made sure his signature was on—transferred reve-
nue to those earning below $100,000 per year. In France, President
Emmanuel Macron's government implemented both a furlough
scheme and a short-time work scheme aimed at supporting the
payroll expenses of employers who retained employees rather
than laying them off during the pandemic, as did Pedro Sanchez's

government in Spain. Countries across the globe adopted similar proposals aimed at limiting the economic impact of the pandemic on vulnerable households.

———

NOR DID THE WAR AND THE SUBSEQUENT LANDSLIDE LABOUR VIC-tory usher in a fundamental dissolution of the old social hierarchies as Orwell had hoped. In *The Road to Wigan Pier*, Orwell identified class prejudice as the key impediment to meaningful social reform. As long as middle-class children, including lower-upper-middle-class children like himself, were raised to believe that the lower classes smell, no solidarity of interests could ever emerge between manual and white-collar labourers, no matter how well the former were paid. A "chasmic, impassable" barrier remained between them. It was to that end that Orwell recommended, after nationalization and income redistribution, the abolition of private schooling, which he saw as effectively "a training in class prejudice," and the creation of a universal system of state education. While he recognized that it would be difficult to abolish private education immediately, he argued that the state should start by taking control of private school admissions and "flooding" those schools with talented working-class and lower-middle-class pupils chosen on the grounds of ability and supported by state aid. Elaborating on his proposals, he wrote, movingly, that "talk of 'defending democracy' is nonsense while it is a mere accident of birth that decides whether a gifted child shall or shall not get the education it deserves."

Once the Labour government was elected, Orwell was particularly bitter about its failure to tackle the problem of education. One year into Attlee's first administration, he opined, "In the social set-up there is no symptom by which one could infer that we are not living under a Conservative government. . . . [I]f any effort is really being made to democratise education, it has borne no fruit as yet." There is a heated debate within the historical and educational literature about the failure of the postwar Labour government both to nationalize private schools and to abolish the grammar schools—elite, selective institutions funded by the state, akin to magnet schools in the US—in favor of a uniform system of comprehensive education for all children. The government's detractors (a group that included Orwell), argued then and since that there was enough public and political support for comprehensive education in the immediate aftermath of the war to enable the government to do away with both private and grammar schools. The government itself thought otherwise. Instead, it prioritized the provision of free school meals. Like Orwell, the government recognized that, first and foremost, "A human being is primarily a bag for putting food into," and without proper nutrition, young people would lack the fortitude to succeed in school. The Attlee government also raised the school-leaving age from fourteen to fifteen in 1947, and ensured that those elite educational institutions, and the ultimate access to university education that they offered, were more open to meritorious working-class pupils.

These were important reforms, but Orwell's conviction that the abolition of the class system was unlikely to occur as long as the two-tiered system of education persisted proved prescient. At the time of writing, over sixty percent of the ministers in Prime Minister Rishi Sunak's cabinet were privately educated—a figure nearly double that of the last two Labour prime ministers, Gordon Brown and Tony Blair. Yet, given that only seven percent of

British children attend private schools, the figure for Blair and Brown's cabinets—thirty-two percent—still meant that the privately educated were massively overrepresented at the top tiers of New Labour government.

Yet, access to higher education *has* been vastly democratized in postwar Britain, compared to previous periods, as it has across the West. The combination of the expansion of the number of students going on to university and the diversification of the backgrounds of university pupils has been one of the most dramatic social transformations of the postwar period. In 1920, when Orwell was a student at Eton, only 4,357 bachelor's degrees were issued in the United Kingdom, three-quarters of them to men. Notably, Orwell's first wife, Eileen O'Shaughnessy Blair, was among the tiny minority of British women to attend university in the 1920s. She earned a bachelor's degree from St. Hugh's College, Oxford, in 1927 and went on to enroll in a master's program in psychology at University College London. In contrast, Orwell himself did not perceive a university degree as necessary to maintain his class standing. Eton was enough.

By 2021, the number of British students entering university had risen nearly three-hundred-fold to 1.29 million, with significantly more women earning degrees than men. Slightly over ninety percent of British university students attended state schools, suggesting that neither gender nor class background is today a significant barrier to entering higher education. Yet, at Oxford and Cambridge—the elite institutions that continue to produce a disproportionate number of MPs, doctors, barristers, and bankers—privately educated pupils continue to be significantly overrepresented. Similar trends persist in the United States, where only two percent of children attend private schools, but private-schoolchildren make up roughly a quarter of Ivy League students. In recent years, "only" around fifteen percent of US senators held bachelor's degrees from the Ivy League—a comparatively modest figure until you take into account that the Ivy League institutions produce 0.4 percent of American university graduates.

So, Orwell had it right about the importance of educational equality, the primacy of which he placed significantly higher than the abolition of the hereditary House of Lords in his agenda for social leveling. At the same time, after weighing the pros and cons, he decided to privately educate his adopted son, Richard, and at first even considered putting him down for that bastion of snobbery, Eton. In October 1948, when Richard was only four, Orwell wrote to his friend Julian Symons that his son's educational future was "a difficult question. . . . Obviously it is democratic for everyone to go to the same schools, . . . but when you see what the elementary schools are like, and the results, you feel that any child that has the chance should be rescued from them." His is a rationalization that remains in frequent use today. To take only two examples, Diane Abbott, a hard-left member of Britain's Labour Party, drew ire from her supporters for enrolling her son at the tony City of London School, and Barack Obama sent his daughters to Sidwell Friends, Washington, DC's most elite prep school. Orwell went on to recall a 1936 meeting with a fellow Old Etonian, John Strachey, who would go on to sit in Attlee's cabinet. Strachey told Orwell that he had enrolled his son at Eton. When Orwell expressed shock at his decision, the former Communist fellow traveler replied that, "given our existing society it was the best education." Orwell reflected, "I don't feel sure that he was wrong"—a double negative that reveals his moral ambivalence about the decision. Orwell and Strachey's own unwillingness to take the leap of faith and enroll their middle-class sons in a state school underscores the entrenched prejudices that the Labour government faced in seeking to reform education.

In the end, Attlee's postwar government decided to focus its energy on less controversial goals, leaving the private school system largely untouched. This failure to seize the moment for farther-reaching change would come back to haunt Britain with the arrival of COVID and lockdown. The pandemic exposed the persistence of the profound inequities in educational resources and attainment that Orwell had highlighted decades earlier, as schools struggled to mitigate the impact of mandatory closures on pupils. When and how schools should reopen for in-classroom teaching quickly became one of the most divisive and hotly contested issues after the onset of the pandemic, with some countries, including France, reopening schools before the end of the 2019–20 school year. Schools in the UK and in several US states returned to in-person teaching (with or without mask mandates) in September 2020, whereas some US school districts—including my children's district in Montgomery County, Maryland—did not resume full-time in-classroom teaching until September 2021. Those who advocated for the early reopening of schools were not only COVID deniers, but also parents, educators, and others who argued that virtual schooling was having a negative impact on all pupils, and a particularly catastrophic impact on children from a lower socioeconomic background.

The pivot to online teaching during the pandemic exhibited the disparities in access to computers, the internet, and private spaces at home in which to participate in online learning. That meant some students thrived (or at least survived) online, while others struggled. Several studies conducted by organizations such as the

Pew Research Center in the United States and the Child Poverty
Action Group and the Education Endowment Foundation in the
UK reported significantly higher rates of learning loss for lower-
income students. These private studies bolstered the conclusions
of the US and UK governments about the differential impact of the
pandemic on students in public and private education.

A report produced by England's Office of Qualifications and
Examinations Regulation (Ofqual) looked specifically at the research
on students attending state-maintained schools and concluded that
students in private schools did much better and tended to receive a
full day of synchronous online tuition (that is, a "live" class taught
over Zoom or another virtual platform) and to have homework
assigned and assessed. The differences in the effect on the schools
was dramatic. "By March 2021, once students had returned to
school, around 8% of independent [private] secondary school teachers reported all or a majority of students were behind in their learning, compared to 40% of teachers in the most deprived schools."

The closure of classrooms during the pandemic also focused
public attention on their continued importance in the nutritional lives of disadvantaged children. While neoliberal spending
reforms had seen the withdrawal of subsidies for school lunches in
Britain and many US states, the most disadvantaged children still
looked to the school cafeteria to secure their nutritional needs.
Campaigns by activists, including, most prominently, the England and Manchester United footballer Marcus Rashford, focused
public attention on the importance of school meals and spurred
governments to take seriously the implications of school cafeteria closures for children who usually receive free school meals.
The campaign spearheaded by Rashford led to the government
committing to provide free school meals during school holiday

closures, and to expand access to free school meals to refugee children and other economically needy groups traditionally ineligible for FSM benefits. In the US, under the Biden administration, the federal government subsidized the provision of free school meals to *all* US schoolchildren during the 2021–22 school year.

An observer in spring 2020 might easily have thought, mistakenly, that the social solidarity engendered by the pandemic would be the beginning of another sea change in the relationship between citizens and the state in key parts of the Western world. Like Orwell in 1940, they might have been convinced that socialism had finally gone from being an abstract theory to a realizable policy. Yet, even before the pandemic restrictions had come to an end, the tidal wave of social legislation unleashed across the West had begun to recede. At the time, such measures had broad popular support, but, as with the Second World War, even before the moment of peril had fully passed, we had begun to return to politics as usual.

In Britain, backbench MPs began to call for an end to furlough payments within months of the scheme's implementation on the grounds that, as Sir Desmond Swayne put it, there was "no such thing as a money tree." In the US, those men and women (and particularly single mothers) who had ended up receiving more in COVID unemployment and stimulus benefits than they had earned in poorly paid service jobs were blamed for undermining the economic recovery and spurring wage inflation when they failed to rejoin the labor market. Such individuals were presented as shirkers when, in reality, many faced COVID-induced childcare constraints or earned so little that they could not justify the health and safety risks of returning to work in industries where their risk of exposure was frequently high.

In March 2021, with the Omicron variant raging throughout the US, millions of schoolchildren learning from home, and
indoor dining only recently reopened in New York City, President
Biden could barely muster enough support to pass his American
Rescue Plan. The bill squeaked through the House of Representa-
tives and Senate without a single Republican vote. The national
program for free school meals in the United States ended in September 2022, even before the US officially declared the pandemic
at an end on April 10, 2023. Biden has announced his commitment to universal free school meals, citing studies that show such
schemes reap dividends in terms of child welfare and educational
performance, but he lacks the political coalition to pass legislation. Only New York City and the states of California, Colorado,
and Maine have maintained the free school meal programs introduced during the pandemic.

In Britain, the mayor of London, Sadiq Khan, took the unprecedented step of expanding the free school meal program to cover
all London schoolchildren in 2023–24, but the unilateral action
of the London government ran contrary to policy at the national
level. The concession that Rashford wrested from the British government in 2020 to provide free school meals to qualified children
over school holidays was not renewed in 2021. As rising interest
rates, put in place by central banks concerned with the rapid rate
of inflation, add to the cost of government borrowing, legislators
and executives around the globe are looking for opportunities to
cut welfare spending. Short-term economies are being privileged
over long-term investments, with the result that social welfare
programs introduced during the pandemic are being cut, even
though all indications suggest that their long-term benefits outweigh their costs.

SIMILAR TO THE FAILURE TO ABOLISH PRIVATE EDUCATION, entrenched sentiment and warring priorities both mediated against the Attlee government taking any action to abolish the House of Lords. In *The Lion and the Unicorn*, Orwell predicted that the postwar socialist government whose coming he saw as inevitable would likely do away with the House of Lords while maintaining the monarchy. In practice, it did neither, despite the frequent calls by Labour politicians for the abolition of both institutions in the 1920s and 1930s. Attempts to reform the House of Lords to make it more representative have been limited. Life peers were not created until 1958, and the right of hereditary peers to sit in the Lords remained inviolate until Tony Blair's government passed the House of Lords Act of 1999. Like Eton, which over the centuries has educated countless lords and monarchs, these two organs of vested privilege were not swept away in a revolutionary fervor.

It is an open question as to what Orwell would have thought about the coronation of King Charles III on May 6, 2023. On one level, he would likely have been surprised that the monarchy has lasted as long as it has. Writing during the Second World War, he purported that royal sentiment, in his judgment, was "much weakened" since the passing of King George V (who reigned from 1910 through 1936), such that it was not even clear whether it was "still a reality in England." On the other hand, in the same article, he argued that the monarch might serve as a useful "escape-valve" for Britons' instincts toward leader worship. Better to adulate "some figure who has no real power," a "waxwork . . . creature who rides in a gilded coach behind soldiers in steel breastplates" than to fixate on a Hitler or a Stalin—or, he might have said today, a Vladimir Putin or a Donald Trump.

WHILE ORWELL'S PROGRAM FOR DEMOCRATIC SOCIALISM BEGAN at home, much of it was directed outward, toward the empire. The *Lion and the Unicorn* called for "immediate Dominion status for India, with power to secede when the war is over." As the second half of Orwell's proposal indicates, dominion status was not the same as independence, as India would still remain tied to the British crown. Nonetheless, it was further than anyone in Britain's wartime coalition government was prepared to go. In March 1942, a year after Orwell published *The Lion and the Unicorn*, Sir Stafford Cripps, then leader of the House of Commons, undertook a mission to India in which he proposed that, in exchange for India's loyalty in the war effort, the British would grant the subcontinent dominion status *once the war was over*. Full independence for India was not discussed. The leaders of the Hindu-dominated Indian National Congress (INC) rejected Cripps's proposals and launched the Quit India movement later that year, which demanded that the British immediately withdraw from the subcontinent. By that point, Orwell appears to have come around to the view that immediate independence for India was inevitable if the war were to be won, albeit independence on terms that included "some kind of trade agreement allowing for a reasonable safe-guarding of British interests." The government, which saw the British Raj as a crucial bulwark against Japanese ambitions in the East, refused to engage with the INC's demands, and the majority of the congress's leadership was imprisoned for the duration of the war.

The lack of constructive dialogue between the INC's leadership and the British Labour movement created a policy vacuum when Labour ultimately came to power in July 1945, and con-

tributed to the government's hasty decision to withdraw from the
subcontinent on August 15, 1947, leaving behind a chaotic political situation that soon developed into a bloody civil war. This
was very much not the path toward independence that Orwell
had envisaged.

The contradictions of Orwell's imperial politics, particularly
vis-à-vis independence, offer an enduring insight into the origins
of ongoing debates over what the former imperial powers owe to
the Global South. In *Burmese Days*, written not long after Orwell
left the Raj, he expressed a clear contempt for the "white man's
burden" argument that the white races had a paternalistic obligation to govern over those they considered "less developed races."
(Rudyard Kipling wrote his famous poem "White Man's Burden"
in 1899 to justify the US occupation of the Philippines.) In *Burmese Days*, Orwell ironically has the Muslim Dr. Veraswami ven-
triloquize the arguments in favor of imperialism: "My friend, it iss
pathetic to me to hear you talk so. . . . [The Burmese] are helpless
without you. . . . [Y]our officials are civilizing us, elevating us to
their level, from pure public spirit. It is a magnificent record of
self-sacrifice." (The "iss" here isn't a typo, but Orwell's rendering
of Dr. Veraswami's lisp, a racial caricature intended, as with the
physical descriptions of Dr. Veraswami discussed in chapter 2, to
render his character foolish.)

The response of Flory, the white British protagonist of Orwell's
tale, is a contemptuous "Bosh!" "We've never taught a single useful
manual trade to the Indians. We daren't; frightened of the compe-
tition in industry. We've even crushed various industries. Where
are the Indian muslins now. . . . The only Eastern races that have
developed at all quickly are the independent ones." Compare this
to Orwell's argument against immediate independence for India

as articulated in *The Lion and the Unicorn*, in which he argues that independence "would be a disaster for India no less than for England. Intelligent Indians know this. As things are at present, India not only cannot defend itself, it is hardly even capable of feeding itself. The whole administration of the country depends on a framework of experts (engineers, forest officers, railwaymen, soldiers, doctors) who are predominantly English and could not be replaced within five or ten years."

When Orwell wrote *Burmese Days* in the 1930s, shortly after leaving the Indian Police Service, he was flush with rage against what he perceived to be the iniquitous imperial system, and focused on the imperative to get the British out of the subcontinent with little or no consideration of the practicalities of how such a departure would be achieved. Nearly a decade later, Orwell found himself walking a difficult tightrope in terms of his politics toward India. He remained acutely conscious that the British had unjustifiably exploited India for centuries—one current estimate calculates the total value of wealth drained from the British Raj at $45 trillion—and that the calls for Britain to leave the subcontinent were justified, but he was increasingly conflicted over whether it was better for India (never mind better for Britain) for the two to make a clear break from one another. Would India develop more quickly if it were independent, as he has Flory contend, or did the British owe it to India to maintain their presence in the region while Indians prepared for self-government? Was the latter contention simply the racist condescension of the "white man's burden," or was it a recognition that, in the short term, the imperial powers owed a debt to the countries that they had intentionally exploited and left underdeveloped?

These are questions that remain with us today, as the United

States and European powers continue to debate their obligations to the Global South. In 1997, Britain's New Labour government established the Department for International Development and committed the country to invest 0.7 percent of gross national income in overseas development aid, the vast majority of which went to states that had formerly been under British imperial control. In 2020, then prime minister Boris Johnson announced that the department would be subsumed under the Foreign and Commonwealth Office and that investment in development aid would be pared back to 0.5 percent of national income. Over the past several years, an increasing share of this reduced aid has never left the United Kingdom, being directed to fund the resettlement of international refugees within the British Isles.

During his presidency, Donald Trump similarly scaled back overseas aid as a percentage of US government spending, a cut that was subsequently reversed by the Biden administration. Trump accompanied his announcement of proposed foreign aid spending for 2021 with a retweet of one of his private tweets from 2014: "I hope we never find life on other planets because there's no doubt that the U.S. Government will start sending them money!" Trump's tweet implied that the recipients of US aid have as little connection to the United States as alien life forms, but, as with other major aid donors, the US gives a significant portion of its foreign aid to countries whose economic woes can be traced back to American imperial legacies of exploitation and underdevelopment.

The formal imperial structures that bound much of the Global South to Europe and the United States in Orwell's lifetime are largely dismantled. The British Empire has gone from covering a quarter of the globe to consisting of a handful of countries in the Caribbean. France left Algeria in 1962. The United States withdrew from the Philippines in 1946. And, while the formal US occupation of Cuba ended in 1902, Fidel Castro effectively ended America's informal occupation of the country in 1959. Yet, the difficult questions of how to atone for the injuries endured by former imperial possessions remains with us. Orwell's optimism that the institutions of empire would give way to a system first of benign tutelage and ultimately of equal partnership has not come to pass.

If the retreat of the shadow cast by the pandemic has revealed the limits of the commitment to investment in social welfare in the West, the pandemic crisis also once again laid bare the limits of Western internationalism. During the Second World War, Orwell had emphasized the need for an international alliance against fascism, in which the "coloured peoples" of the British Empire and "China, Abyssinia and all other victims of the Fascist powers" would be treated as equal partners with the Western democracies. Instead, the end of the war instantiated the political power of the West, as the old League of Nations was replaced by the United Nations, with a permanent security council dominated by Western powers.

Eighty-five years later, the US and British governments invested millions in the development of the Pfizer-BioNTech, Moderna, and AstraZeneca vaccines, with obvious benefit to humanity. Yet, when it came time to mass-produce and distribute the vaccine doses, Western governments engaged in what became known as "vaccine nationalism." In February 2021, the director-general of the World Health Organization, Tedros Adhanom Ghebreyesus, wrote in *Foreign Policy* that, "at present, rich countries with just 16 percent of the world's population have bought up 60 percent of the world's vaccine supply." He noted that it was the goal of the richer nations to vaccinate over two-thirds of their populations by midyear, with the aim of achieving herd immunity. By contrast, COVAX—the multilateral organization tasked with providing vaccines to the Global South—was struggling to obtain enough supply to vaccinate even twenty percent of the population of the world's poorest nations by the end of 2021. Developments in the months that followed—not least the emergence of a large-scale campaign of vaccine skepticism that meant many Americans, in particular, declined to be vaccinated—did mean that the West ended up donating more doses of vaccine than planned to the developing world. Yet, as of July 2023, the number of doses the US had shipped abroad was roughly equivalent to the number of doses administered to its own citizens—a figure that may initially seem high, but falls short of expectations of the world's wealthiest country and largest pharmaceutical producer.

———

JUST AS THE PANDEMIC SEEMED TO SHINE A SUDDEN LIGHT ON systemic disparities between rich and poor people, communities, and countries, it also highlighted gendered disparities in the impact of both the virus and the resultant lockdowns on individuals and households. Again, the experience of the pandemic recalled the ghost of the Second World War, which had brought into the spotlight long-festering inequities in the relationship between men and women in Allied society. During the Second World War, the state made exceptional demands of its female citizens in both the US and UK. Rosie the Riveter—the allegorical representation of US women's physical contribution to the war effort as factory laborers—has earned a place in popular memory and iconography, thanks largely to J. Howard Miller's 1943 "We Can Do It!" poster, originally produced for display in Westinghouse Electric's munitions factories, but since immortalized on US postage stamps and commodified on T-shirts, coffee mugs, and countless products for sale on Etsy. But, as with the wartime British government's equally commodified "Keep Calm and Carry On" poster, the optimistic slogan masks the extent of social disruption engendered by the US government's call to mothers and daughters to take on the work of absent husbands, brothers, and fathers on the factory floor, while still finding time to manage their childcare and other domestic responsibilities.

Women played an even more central role in the war effort in Britain, where the home front was under physical attack from bombers and so thoroughly mobilized. Churchill's December 1941 National Service Act allowed for the conscription of unmarried women and childless widows for war work. Although not conscripted, married women and mothers were expected to do their part for the war effort, albeit frequently without the same compensation as their male counterparts. (In her biography of Orwell's first wife, Eileen Blair, Sylvia Topp mentions an internal memorandum from the Ministry of Information, where Eileen worked in everything but title as a private secretary, although on a typist's salary: "If and when she is replaced by a man Private Secretary a suitable salary + allowance should be fixed.") The government opened temporary nurseries around the country to enable women with young children to work outside of the home. By the war's end, women made up over one-third of Britain's industrial workforce. The Labour feminist Ellen Wilkinson, one of the most senior women in Churchill's administration, took a controversial stand as Minister of Home Security when she insisted that women should do their share of work as fire watchers as well, on the grounds that, as equal citizens, they should have equal obligations. While some women resented the obligation, tens of thousands went beyond the call of duty, volunteering to work as air wardens, ambulance drivers, and canteen and relief workers during the Blitz.

Yet, the suggestion that women were now equal citizens was not realized either during or after the war. As with Eileen Blair, women were paid less than men for comparable labor during the conflict. When the Attlee government commenced its project of building the postwar welfare state, these working women hoped that the New Jerusalem would take them into account. Yet, claims for equal pay were fobbed off by Labour's chancellors as unaffordable; wartime day nurseries were shuttered as married women were encouraged to leave the workforce and return to child-rearing; and women's presumed dependency on a male breadwinner was instantiated in the terms of the new state pension system, which classed women workers separately from men and afforded them lower benefits.

The double standards infuriated many feminists, but apparently did not bother Orwell. While both his first and his second wife worked, as did most of his girlfriends over the years, he accepted as natural that women should be the primary caregivers. After they married, his first wife, Eileen, put her own career ambitions as a psychology student on hold to effectively become his amanuensis, tending his home, while typing, editing, and proofreading his work. After her death, he brought his sister Avril—who had helped pick up after young Eric while he mooched around his parents' house in Southwold writing *Down and Out*—to live with him and care for his adopted son, Richard. During the final years of his life, Orwell was vocal in criticizing the Labour government's failings, but not once did he suggest that it should have done more to support working women.

Another inequality that the pandemic exposed and deepened, but which legislators did almost nothing to combat, was the continued gender imbalance in care work between women and men, mothers and fathers, daughters and sons. When schools and daycare centers closed, and home visits stopped to older citizens and others in the community with social care needs, women bore a disproportionate share of the burden of both child and elder care. Just as women's gender-specific concerns had remained marginal to government policy in the 1940s, during the COVID-19 pandemic, Western governments failed to target relief policies specifically at women workers. According to UN data, caring burdens caused women to leave the labor force in disproportionately high numbers during the first year of the pandemic. Economists are predicting that, even if these women ultimately return to the workforce, the temporary withdrawal of female labor will have long-term impacts on the gender pay gap. Perhaps it's no coincidence that the relatively progressive, interventionist domestic policies of the lockdown era and the in-many-ways-revolutionary Orwell seem to have had the exact same blind spot: gender injustice.

WRITING IN 1941, ORWELL BELIEVED THAT THE UNIQUE CIRCUM-stances of the Second World War had created an opening for radical social change in Britain and the fundamental restructuring of Britain's empire. Despite his rhetoric of "peacefully if possible, violently if necessary," all evidence suggests that he believed that the new "English Revolution" could be achieved democratically, in a transformation more akin to the Glorious Revolution of 1688 than the American Revolution that won the thirteen colonies independence from the British crown a century later. At the time that Orwell wrote, Britain was experiencing an exceptional degree of social cohesion, forged in part through the shared experience of the Blitz, a cohesion that played a significant role in Labour's landslide victory four years later.

Admittedly, the postwar welfare states fell considerably short of the full-blown social revolution that Orwell had prophesized in 1941. Yet, as we've seen over the past several years, much of Orwell's analysis of the problems of and remedies for 1940s Britain remain exceptionally relevant to our modern era.

The world has changed dramatically since Orwell published *The Lion and the Unicorn* in 1941. Technological progress and the attendant growth of the global economy have raised millions out of absolute poverty, while greater government involvement in national and individual well-being during the war was made permanent by the postwar welfare states, however reduced they may be today. Yet, the social ills with which Orwell diagnosed Britain in the early days of the war remain prevalent.

Was there, in fact, a missed opportunity during either the Second World War or the recent pandemic to sustain the social cohesion that existed at the height of the crisis and usher in a permanent democratic renegotiation of the social contract toward the type of egalitarian society Orwell envisaged? (Or one even more truly equal than Orwell imagined?)

Orwell's death in January 1950 makes it impossible to guess how his politics would have developed during the decades of the Cold War. We don't know whether the threat to liberty posed by Stalinism and Maoism would have come to weigh more heavily on him than the threat posed by laissez-faire capitalism, which, he argued in a 1944 review of Friedrich Hayek's *A Road to Serfdom*, "means for the great mass of people a tyranny probably worse, because more irresponsible, than that of the State." Yet, the possibility that Orwell would have privileged the Cold War against foreign tyranny over the class war at home does not detract from the value of his social criticism to those looking to understand the history and endurance of inequality on both a state and an international level. Nor does it discredit his proposed model for a democratic socialist revolution. Rather, it pushes us to ask whether the types of revolutionary changes in the balance of wealth and power that Orwell advocated for would indeed make for a better world, whether the democratic socialist revolution that Orwell envisaged in 1941 is, in fact, within our grasp, and whether it could succeed without risking the loss of liberty and descent into tyranny that Orwell feared.

Afterword

FOR FREEDOM'S SAKE

The Western world has changed dramatically in the nearly seventy-five years since Orwell's death, including in ways that reveal some significant progress between Orwell's era and our own. The Cold War is over. Decolonization has brought an end to the overseas empires that characterized the global power system of his youth, and the emergence of the European Union has (hopefully) ushered in an end to nationalist conflict between its member states. Civil rights and second- and third-wave feminist movements have critiqued and are trying to redefine who has access to power and a voice in political and social decision-making. And, perhaps most strikingly, the invention of the internet has led to a radical restructuring of society's relationship to information that has simultaneously empowered individuals and increased the surveillance capabilities of the state and of corporations in ways arguably foreshadowed in *Nineteen Eighty-Four*. Finally, the salience of climate change and concerns over the future of the environment were alien to Orwell, but have become central to political debate in the twenty-first century. If Orwell's generation accepted pollution as an inevitable, if unpleasant, by-product of industrial progress— with Londoners grimly referring to the polluted city air as "pea soup"—we are now conscious of the long-term impact of fossil fuels on our climate, and coalitions committed to green industry and development are gaining strength.

Yet, even as the world has changed, many of the core problems that Orwell identified in his own time continue to haunt us in the twenty-first century. Most crucially, the tension between individual liberty and social solidarity, which Orwell consistently identified in his political writing, remains with us globally.

Orwell is justly admired for his grasp of the essential truth that tyranny is incompatible with liberty. There is no such thing as a benevolent dictatorship, he taught us, whether it be a dictatorship of the left or of the right, or the "white man's burden" of imperial dictatorship. Writing in 1946, Orwell attributed the desire to become an author in part to a "historical impulse," or the "[d]esire to see things as they are, to find out true facts and store them up for the use of posterity." He was committed to recording the truth of history as he saw it. Even *Nineteen Eighty-Four* was, in a sense, an exercise in truth telling, in that it was an effort to open readers' eyes to the existential threats to truth, and thereby to freedom, posed by all-powerful states.

———

THE DYSTOPIAN VISION THAT ORWELL DEPICTED IN *NINETEEN Eighty-Four* has not yet materialized, even in the most authoritarian regimes. While the worst excesses of state surveillance and disinformation have been limited to non-Western states such as Putin's Russia and Xi's China, the West has not been immune from such threats. Ironically, it is not government bureaucrats operating out of state-run Minitrues, but large multinational companies such as Meta and the X Corporation (formerly Twitter Inc.) that present the biggest threat to freedom of information in the West. Further, despite the seeming triumph of Western democracy over Soviet communism at the end of the twentieth century, the rise of populist regimes in the West has threatened the sanctity of democratic liberties in countries from the United States and Brazil in the Americas to Hungary and Poland in the European Union. At the same time, inequality and its impact both on individuals and on societies more generally is again at the fore of debate among politicians and policymakers. And, for all the progress pioneered by feminism, our current gender order, with its implicit and continuing assumptions of women's lesser status and rights as citizens, betrayed by persistent scandals like the gender pay gap and the extremely low prosecution rates for sexual assault, would not seem wholly alien to a visitor from the 1940s.

What would Orwell have thought about the persistence of tyranny and inequality alongside the apparent failure of socialism in the twenty-first century? Arguably, he would not have been surprised.

Orwell wanted a better, more equal, and socially just world. At the same time, he wanted a world in which the personal liberties and individual freedoms that he valued so highly were safeguarded. He believed it was necessary for the state to protect its citizens from poverty and want, but that it should also secure their freedom of thought and action. For a brief moment early in the war, Orwell was overcome by an uncharacteristic optimism that Britain could achieve the level of social revolution he desired without the bureaucratic overreach that he feared. That optimism quickly waned as he realized that there wasn't popular support for a democratic revolution, and that there were those on the left who were looking to the command economy and unaccountable bureaucracy of the Soviet Union as a model for Britain. As I've said earlier, he wrote *Animal Farm* and *Nineteen Eighty-Four* to make crystal clear that the brutally enforced collectivism of the Soviet Union and its satellite regimes did not offer true equality.

Nineteen Eighty-Four, in particular, is one of the most pessimistic examples of dystopian fiction ever published. Throughout 1947 and 1948, as Labour's minister of health and housing, Anuerin "Nye" Bevan, fought a ferocious battle with the British Medical Association over the impending implementation of the National Health Service, Orwell labored over *Nineteen Eighty-Four* on the Scottish island of Jura. It was a race against time. He was already suffering horribly from the tuberculosis that would kill him only eighteen months after the NHS came into existence. His physical pain may or may not have informed the intense psychic pain that pervades the novel. At the time he wrote *Nineteen Eighty-Four*, Orwell was concerned that, lacking a democratic mandate for reform, the government could turn to the machinery of an overreaching state bureaucracy to achieve its ends, with dangerous consequences for English liberty. He makes his concerns clear through the character of Emmanuel Goldstein: "Socialism . . . was still deeply infected by the Utopianism of past ages. But in each variant of Socialism that appeared from about 1900 onwards the aim of establishing liberty and equality was more and more openly abandoned." Utopia in *Nineteen Eighty-Four* is exposed as a fantasy. In the world of Oceania, the socialist meritocracy that replaced the old aristocracy of wealth proved to be as rigid and unequal as its predecessor. Hereditary privilege persisted, only now it was the children of meritocrats who increasingly filled the classrooms of Eton.

Nineteen Eighty-Four is a bleak book, with a bleak ending. Its final scene is chilling. The book spoke to the anxieties of the time, anxieties that remain with us in the twenty-first century. But Orwell was not solely, or even primarily, a pessimistic writer. As he insisted, *Nineteen Eighty-Four* was a warning, not a prophecy. "I do not believe that the kind of society I describe necessarily *will* arrive, but I believe (allowing of course for the fact that the book is a satire) that something resembling it *could* arrive. I believe also that totalitarian ideas have taken root in the minds of intellectuals everywhere." Taken as a body, Orwell's writing offers a road map for how to resist the temptations of totalitarianism in favor of a more open and democratic socialism.

———

BY NOW, SEVERAL GENERATIONS OF READERS HAVE DISCOVERED the value of Orwell's work as a lens through which to gain clarity on both the recent past and the evolving present. What facet of Orwell's multidimensional legacy readers have focused on has varied with their own politics and with their historical and geopolitical circumstances. In the immediate aftermath of his death, Orwell was eulogized as an iconoclastic socialist by his peers in Britain, a rebel committed to facing unpleasant truths, not least about the nature of Soviet totalitarianism, but equally dedicated to the project of social revolution. His friend, the novelist and critic V. S. Pritchett, writing in the *New Statesman and Nation*, declared Orwell to be "the wintry conscience of a generation which in the 'thirties had heard the call to the rasher assumptions of political faith." By this he meant that Orwell had not allowed himself to be lulled into a false sense of complacency by the promises of either fascistic nationalism or Soviet communism. He always knew the importance of truth and liberty, and was unwilling to sacrifice either on the mantle of communitarian ideology. As Pritchett argued, "He prided himself on seeing through the rackets, and on conveying the impression of living without the solace or even the need of a single illusion."

It was a lonely life, and one that invariably alienated Orwell from the majority of the political left with which he consistently identified. Yet Pritchett saw a nobility, almost a saintliness, in his unerring honesty. Orwell's personal integrity and the honesty of his writing were remarked upon again and again in the days following his death. To the *Times* of London, he was "a writer of acute and penetrating temper and of conspicuous honesty of mind." Although the *Times* remained a center-right newspaper, it was able to appreciate the politics of a man who "made no bones about the primary need of securing social justice," and lamented that "the death of so searching and sincere a writer is a very real loss." Writing in the *Observer*, Arthur Koestler praised his integrity and noted that "his uncompromising intellectual honesty was such that it made him appear almost inhuman at times." He was a "true" rebel, who rejected the "emotionally shallow Leftism" of many intellectuals in the 1930s in favor of his own iconoclastic brand of "social revolt." The *Manchester Guardian* classed him as an "intellectual Socialist who preached that socialism, to have any meaning, must be uncompromisingly wedded to democracy and ordinary life." For his admirers in Britain, Orwell represented a model of how to toe a politically honest line through a world beset by corruption and false promises.

Already, however, his reputation in the United States had started to take on a different cast. Crucially, neither *The Road to Wigan Pier* nor *Homage to Catalonia* appeared in the US during his lifetime, and both *Burmese Days* and *Down and Out in Paris and London* had been released in America to little fanfare. The *New York Times*'s obituary included the subheading "Two Novels Popular Here," and noted that, while he was considered in the UK to be one of the "leading British novelists of the day," in the US his reputation rested almost entirely on *Animal Farm* and *Nineteen Eighty-Four*. Most of the other large dailies carried an Associated Press obituary, which merely identified him as the author of *Nineteen Eighty-Four*, which over the preceding year had reached number three on US bestseller lists. Americans' limited familiarity with Orwell's work beyond those two late novels inevitably gave them a different perspective on the author, one more attuned to his uncompromising stand against Stalinism, and they were less conscious of his abhorrence of social injustice. It is not surprising that, in July 1949, Orwell felt compelled to write a letter to an American reader (later excerpted in *Life* magazine and the *New York Times Book Review*) in which he made clear that he was a supporter of Britain's Labour government. The *New York Times* obituary, like those in the British press, emphasized his "burning passion for truth," but was more skeptical about his position on the political spectrum, noting that he "showed an unconventional attitude towards left-wing politics" and "curiously . . . he considered himself a Marxist and a member of the non-communist left wing of the British Labour party." (Whether Orwell considered himself a Marxist is doubtful. He professed—although many have doubted him—not to have read Marx. His wife Eileen once joked to a friend that the couple had named their poodle Marx "to remind us that we have never read Marx, [but] now we have a read a little and taken so strong a personal dislike to the man that we can't look the dog in the face.")

Before his death, Orwell had made sure to arrange for *Animal Farm* to be translated into Polish and Ukrainian. In the years that followed, both official and samizdat editions of *Animal Farm* and *Nineteen Eighty-Four* were produced in nearly every Central and Eastern European language and circulated clandestinely behind the Iron Curtain. For those living under Soviet tyranny, Orwell became a symbol of opposition and for the defense of truth. As the Polish dissident author Czesław Miłosz wrote in the early 1950s, Orwell held an immense fascination for those living under Stalinism. "Even those who know Orwell only by hearsay are amazed that a writer who never lived in Russia should have so keen a perception into its life." His appeal to opponents of the Soviet Union and other forms of totalitarianism should not be understated. Yet, the broader public's association of Orwell primarily with *Animal Farm* and *Nineteen Eighty-Four* meant that few appreciated the complexity of his political commitment. Orwell the cold warrior lacked the nuance that defined Orwell the man.

With time, while he continued to be near deified behind the Iron Curtain, Western readers began to move away from the idea of Orwell the prophet and to read his final dystopian novel as a commentary on the evolution of their own society. In 1961, Erich Fromm, the German-born psychoanalyst who fled Nazi Germany for the United States in the 1930s, wrote an afterword for the Signet Classic edition of *Nineteen Eighty-Four* (the same edition I read in high school) that argued that the Western powers were as susceptible to the manipulations of doublethink as Russia and China. He conceded that, in penning the concept of "double-

think," Orwell had in mind the specific manipulations of Soviet
communism, which he saw pursuing ends anathema to socialism
by decidedly unsocialist means. Yet, Fromm argued that the Cold
War West, too, had succumbed to doublethink: "We present our
society as being one of free initiative, individualism and ideal-
ism, when in reality these are mostly words. We are a central-
ized managerial industrial society, of an essentially bureaucratic
nature, and motivated by a materialism which is only slightly mit-
igated by truly spiritual or religious concerns." For the generation
of 1968, which protested American involvement in the Vietnam
War as oppressive militarism disguised as liberation for the Viet-
namese, Orwell's doublethink became a way of understanding
US foreign policy. For feminists, the Party's insistence on controlling the citizens of Oceania's sexuality was analogous to the
New Right's determination to restrict abortion. As the *New York
Times* argued in a January 1984 retrospective on the enduring
impact of Orwell's novel, "Many critics view the Reagan admin-
istration's opposition to abortion as the rawest demonstration of
Big Brotherism."

THE END OF THE COLD WAR ONCE AGAIN PROVOKED A RE-
evaluation of the value of Orwell's work, as the direct parallels
between life on *Animal Farm* or in Big Brother's Oceania faded
with Mikhail Gorbachev's introduction of glasnost in 1985.
Orwell's last two novels continued to have an uncanny verisimili-
tude for China, still ruled by a repressive regime of authoritarian
censorship and surveillance—but for Western readers, Orwell's
significance shifted away from his role as a prophet of the Cold
War. He came to be viewed once again as an iconoclast and a

truth teller—a political chronicler whose principal virtue was his integrity. Christopher Hitchens, himself a self-fashioned political iconoclast, did much to burnish Orwell's reputation in this regard.

It is also the version of George Orwell presented in the iconic Apple Macintosh computer commercial that aired during the Super Bowl in January 1984. Against a backdrop of black-and-white male automatons paying obeisance to Big Brother on a giant telescreen, a Technicolor woman wielding a sledgehammer destroys the telescreen and liberates the transfixed audience—just as the new age of Apple personal computing promised liberation to the individual user. The advertisement is ironic on multiple levels. Orwell was vocal in his dislike of both capitalism and technology (he liked to brag about not owning a radio), and Apple's use of an empowered female athlete to represent its product doesn't exactly draw on Orwell, given his decidedly traditional attitude toward gender roles. On a deeper level, while personal computing has liberated and empowered individual voices, the technological revolution engendered by the rise of PC and mobile technology and the explosion of the internet and social media has created a powerful new information nexus that many perceive as carrying the potential to deliver us into a new Orwellian dystopia.

If we trace the use of the term *Orwellian* in the twenty-first century, it has become inextricably tied to the manipulation of truth and the circulation of disinformation enabled by the internet age. Notably, while print copies of *Animal Farm* and *Nineteen Eighty-Four* are not censored in China, the government does censor online comparisons between Xi's regime and Orwell's fictional worlds—a recognition of the greater political power of online media. The term *Orwellian* has also been tied to a new concern with censorship and the "cancellation" of opinion, both in authoritarian regimes like China, Russia, Afghanistan, and Iran and in democratic societies like the United States. The resurgence of *Nineteen Eighty-Four* in Russia during the Ukraine war is testament to the enduring strength of his message about the power of disinformation and the lie that "War is Peace."

ORWELL'S WORK—NOT ONLY HIS TWO MOST FAMOUS NOVELS, BUT equally *Burmese Days* and essays such as "Politics and the English Language" and "Notes on Nationalism"—have much to offer us today as we weigh the competing demands of truth and tolerance and free speech and fair speech in the internet age. Yet, Orwell can offer even more to the left, if the left takes him as a writer who was determined to chart a political path that would achieve meaningful social equality without sacrificing personal liberty.

In recent years, several prominent thinkers have inserted themselves into the public conversation over the rise of inequality and the persistence of poverty despite unprecedented international wealth in the twenty-first century. Reading their policy prescriptions, it is hard not to be reminded of Orwell's proposals for an English revolution in *The Lion and the Unicorn*. In *Poverty, by America*, the Princeton sociologist Matthew Desmond makes explicit reference to Orwell's depictions of poverty in *The Road to Wigan Pier* as he describes the condition of the modern American poor and calls for government intervention to redistribute surplus wealth in a language reminiscent of wartime Orwell. Thomas Piketty's *A Brief History of Equality* similarly turns to Orwellian prescriptions of the capture and redistribution of wealth by the state to solve the problem of entrenched intergenerational inequality. Notably, in a lengthy essay on the phenomenal success of Pik-

etty's *Capital* in post-2008 America, the *Atlantic* journalist Joe
Pinsker compared Piketty's revulsion against modern inequality to Orwell's critique of the class system in 1940s Britain, refer-
encing an entry from Orwell's wartime diary in which he opined
about the selfishness of the servant-employing classes: "Apparently nothing will ever teach these people that the other 99 percent
of the population exist."

Since the 2008 financial crisis, the intensifying backlash
against the excesses of neoliberalism has led even the staunchest
defenders of liberalism to support the need for the state to blunt
the forces of inequality. In his short treatise *Liberalism and Its
Discontents* (2022), Francis Fukuyama argued that much of the
neoliberals' hostility to government was "simply irrational," and
that all but the most "hardened sociopaths" were influenced by
social norms as well as by individual interest. In defending liberalism as, to paraphrase Winston Churchill, the worst form of
government, excepting all others, Fukuyama underscores the fact
that substantial state intervention in the economy with the aim of
safeguarding individuals from the worst excesses of the market is
compatible with a liberal definition of personal freedom.

Yet, contemporary calls for more aggressive state intervention to address inequality come up against the same fundamental obstacle that Orwell encountered in the 1940s: a lack of social
cohesion that would allow such a level of socioeconomic reform
to be implemented without recourse to state coercion. It is notable
that Orwell thought he had witnessed such cohesion in the early
days of the Spanish Civil War in Barcelona, when masters and
servants had become equals and everyone called each other comrade rather than *señor* or *usted*. But the change, it turned out, was
illusory. Even before he left the country in June 1937, Orwell had

come to realize that "great numbers of well-to-do bourgeois were simply lying low and disguising themselves as proletarians for the time being."

The question then becomes how to prepare a society rent by decades of neoliberal excess to accept a social democratic revolution without resorting to government overreach. And here, Orwell's writing contains an enduring lesson for our modern moment. His body of work emphasizes the importance of finding unity in a shared sense of humanity not rooted in an exclusionary "nationalism" of country, class, politics, race, or religion. In his first published book, *Down and Out in Paris and London*, he emphasized the humanity and integrity of men and women who many were inclined to dismiss as morally complicit in their own poverty. The book is full of sketches of figures like Bozo the scrivener, who, despite being unemployed and homeless and destined for "beggary and a death in the workhouse," had a capacious intellect, had read "some of Zola's novels, all Shakespeare's plays, *Gulliver's Travels*, and a number of essays," and had "managed to keep his brain intact and alert, and so nothing could make him succumb to poverty. He might be ragged and cold, or even starving, but so long as he could read, think, and watch for meteors, he was, as he said, free in his own mind."

Orwell grants these men and women (admittedly, principally men) their dignity, and thereby undermines his readers' capacity to dismiss their suffering. So, too, in his essay "A Hanging" (1931). There, he humanizes a poor Hindi prisoner condemned to hanging by describing his instinctive side step around a puddle as he was being frog-marched to the scaffold. "It is curious," Orwell remarks, "but till that moment I had never realized what it means to destroy a healthy, conscious man. When I saw the prisoner step aside to avoid the puddle, I saw the mystery, the unspeakable wrongness, of cutting a life short when it is in full tide."

In *The Road to Wigan Pier*, he tackles the prejudices of his readers head on, identifying the widely held belief that the unemployed were merely "cynical parasites" living a pampered existence on the dole, and systematically dismantles it through a mountain of testimony to the circumstances in which the readers' fellow citizens live. Despite his reservations about the second section of the book, even Victor Gollancz could appreciate that Orwell's goal was to bridge the vast chasm that separated the working and middle classes. The first section of *The Lion and the Unicorn*, "England Your England," with its patriotic emphasis that what unites the English people is stronger that what divides them, represents the apotheosis of Orwell's belief that, if only we could recognize our shared humanity, we would unite around the need for a social revolution.

Even among the hopelessness of *Nineteen Eighty-Four*, Orwell includes several scenes of poor, downtrodden proletarian women asserting their humanity through song. The sound of one of these women singing in a powerful contralto convinces Winston that, if there is hope, it must lie in the proles.

> The mystical reverence that he felt for her was somehow mixed up with the aspect of the pale, cloudless sky, stretching away behind the chimney-pots into interminable distance. It was curious to think that the sky was the same for everybody, in Eurasia or Eastasia as well as here. And the people under the sky were also very much the same—everywhere, all over the world, hundreds of thousands of millions of people just like this, people ignorant of one

another's existence, held apart by walls of hatred and lies,
and yet almost exactly the same—people who had never
learned to think but who were storing up in their hearts
and bellies and muscles the power that would one day overturn the world.

In recent years, politics across the West has increasingly focused
on exploiting the differences between individuals and groups,
rather than emphasizing their common humanity. This has been
as true on the left as on the right. As with the left-wing "cranks"
of whom Orwell despaired in the 1930s, today's more militant left
too often takes an approach "sufficient to alienate plenty of decent
people." The message of Orwell's writing for those on the left who
would like to see a social revolution achieved in our lifetime is to
reach across the "walls of hatred and lies" that divide us from one
another. Orwell's message is not that socialism is humbug, but
that a democratic socialist revolution—the only type of revolution
worth its salt—can only be achieved through common endeavor.
To quote the farm animals' anthem:

> *For that day we all must labour,*
> *Though we die before it break;*
> *Cows and horses, geese and turkeys.*
> *All must toil for freedom's sake.*

ACKNOWLEDGMENTS

This book owes a debt first and foremost to George Orwell himself. Orwell has long been, and remains, one of my favorite writers and thinkers, his faults notwithstanding. A shared love of Orwell's writing was one of the many things that initially brought my husband and me together. Over the past two years working on this book, I've gotten to know Orwell on a more intimate level, as I've reread many of his more personal essays and worked through several of his biographies with which I had not previously been acquainted. My family, too, owes a debt to Orwell. Inspired by his and Eileen's efforts to run a self-sufficient farm on the land surrounding their cottage in Wallington, Hertfordshire, my boys and I have become suburban farmers, growing sugar snap peas, runner beans, tomatoes, broccoli, peppers, and herbs in raised beds on the front lawn. Last summer, they accompanied me on a trip to Barcelona, and learned an unexpected amount about the history of the Spanish Civil War and Orwell's role in it. Orwell's ghost has joined us at the dinner table and informed our discussions of history and current events.

Second, the book owes a debt to my students, both at the University of Birmingham, where I led a master's seminar on Orwell's writing, and at American University, where I have taught "George Orwell and the Making of the Modern World" for the past three years. Their insights into and perspectives on Orwell's work and its relation to contemporary events shine through throughout this text, particularly in chapter 5. The quickness of my students, both male and female, to identify and call out Orwell's misogynistic tendencies gives me hope for a future less constrained by patriarchal assumptions.

Before *Orwell's Ghosts*, I laid out some of my thoughts on the links between Orwell's writing and our contemporary political reality in two pieces for CNN's opinion section, and I owe a huge debt of gratitude to Jane Carr and Richard Galant for editing and publishing those columns, as their engaged reception persuaded me that there was an appetite for a book on Orwell's enduring legacy. Fortunately, my agent, Andrew Gordon, agreed, and his faith in the project, as well as that of George Lucas, was crucial in ensuring that it ultimately saw the light of day. I was immensely fortunate to be able to work with both Amy Cherry at W. W. Norton and Lara Weisweiller-Wu at Hurst in developing the manuscript. The book is much stronger for their productive collaboration. Research funding from American University allowed me to consult Orwell's papers in the British Library and University College London, and to travel to Barcelona to retrace his and Eileen's time in the city. Chapter 2, in particular, benefited from conversations with my brother Andrew, an expert on political disinformation networks.

Finally, *Orwell's Ghosts* was largely written while my boys, now seven and twelve, and I were based in Bethesda, Maryland, and my husband was teaching in the UK. I am ever grateful to them for their forbearance, and even more grateful to my mom and dad, whose willingness to look after their grandsons helped me carve out the time and space to write and revise the manuscript. The book is dedicated to Alex and Gabe, but *Orwell's Ghosts* belongs as much to Debbie and Don Beers.

Notes

BOOKS BY GEORGE ORWELL PUBLISHED

DURING HIS LIFETIME

Down and Out in Paris and London (1933)
Burmese Days (1934)
A Clergyman's Daughter (1935)
The Road to Wigan Pier (1936)
Keep the Aspidistra Flying (1936)
Homage to Catalonia (1938)
Coming Up for Air (1939)
Inside the Whale, and Other Essays (1940)
The Lion and the Unicorn: Socialism and the English Genius (1941)
Animal Farm (1945)
Critical Essays (1946)
The English People (1947)
Nineteen Eighty-Four (1949)

DEDICATION

7 **"awful fun in spite of the nuisance":** Letter to Julian Symonds, April 20, 1948, Add. Ms. 8890/6/1, British Library, London.

INTRODUCTION: WHAT'S ORWELLIAN?

11 **a new "Ministry of Truth"**: Taylor Lorenz, "How the Biden administration let right-wing attacks derail its disinformation efforts," *Washington Post*, May 18, 2022.

12 **"Orwellian thought policing"**: *303 Creative LLC v. Elenis*, 600 U.S. ____ (2023), slip op. at 20 n. 4 and at 25 (June 30, 2023); Ibid. at 34 n.14 (Sotomayor, J., dissenting).

12 **"Orwell's '1984' and Trump's America"**: Adam Gopnik, "Orwell's '1984' and Trump's America," *The New Yorker*, January 27, 2017.

12 **"inane and Orwellian"**: Rafael Behr, "Inane and Orwellian: A Queen's speech to improve the life of Boris Johnson," *Guardian*, May 10, 2022.

15 **"power of facing unpleasant facts"**: "Why I Write," *Gangrel*, no. 4 (summer 1946), republished on the Orwell Foundation website, accessed June 9, 2023, https://www.orwellfoundation.com/the-orwell-foundation/orwell/essays-and-other-works/why-i-write.

19 **"Break any of these rules"**: "Politics and the English Language," *Horizon*, April 1946, in *The Collected Essays, Journalism and Letters of George Orwell*, ed. Sonia Orwell and Ian Angus, vol. 4, *In Front of Your Nose* (New York: Harcourt, Brace & World, 1968), 139.

19 **"Spring is here"**: "Some Thoughts on the Common Toad," in *Collected Essays*, vol. 4, 144.

1. FROM ERIC BLAIR TO GEORGE ORWELL

23 **Born on June 25, 1903:** Unless otherwise noted, the biographical detail in this chapter can be found in Bernard Crick, *George Orwell: A Life* (London: Secker & Warburg, 1980).

24 **nearly four hundred slaves:** "Charles Blair: Profile & Legacies Summary, 1776–1854," Centre for the Legacies of British Slavery, maintained by University College London, https://www.ucl.ac.uk/lbs/person/view/2146630288.

24 **portrait of Fane, which Eric would later inherit:** Peter Stansky, *The Socialist Patriot: George Orwell and War* (Stanford, CA: Stanford University Press, 2023), 8.

24 **"the [Blair] house is very small"**: Eileen Blair to Norah Myles, November 1936, in *George Orwell: A Life in Letters*, ed. Peter Davison (London: Penguin, 2011), 67.

25 **nasty caricature of the Anglo-Indian household:** *Coming Up for Air* (New York: Harcourt, Brace, 1950 [1939]), 156–57.

26 **"one or two of [his Limouzin]"**: Jacintha Buddicom, *Eric & Us* (London: Finlay, 2006), 14.

27 *"amateur* of detective stories":* Letter to Julian Symonds, February 4, 1949, Add. Ms. 8890/6/1, British Library, London.

28 **"filled me with resentment"**: *The Road to Wigan Pier* (Harmondsworth, UK: Penguin, 1962 [1936]), 120.

28 *"the lower classes smell"*: *Road to Wigan Pier*, 112 (the italics are in the original).

29 **"that the long drilling in patriotism"**: "My Country, Right or Left," in *The Collected Essays, Journalism and Letters of George Orwell*, ed. Sonia Orwell and Ian Angus, vol. 1, *An Age Like This* (New York: Harcourt, Brace & World, 1968), 539.

29 **"a snobbish, expensive public school"**: *Road to Wigan Pier*, 122.

29 **"festering centres of snobbery"**: *The Lion and the Unicorn* (London: Secker & Warburg, 1941), 104.

29 considered sending his adopted son: Jeffrey Meyers, "Orwell: Wintry Conscience of a Generation," *Booknotes*, C-SPAN, February 28, 2001. Available at https://www.c-span.org/video/?c1235572/user-clip-clip-iorwell-wintry-conscience-generation.

29 **"socialist intellectual" as an "Old Etonian"**: *Road to Wigan Pier*, 119.

30 **"As the war fell back into the past"**: "My Country, Right or Left," *Collected Essays*, vol. 1, 537–38.

31 his characteristic **"pounce"**: Graham Bowker, "Blair Pounces," *Times Literary Supplement*, no. 5421, February 23, 2007, 15.

31 decision to join the IPS: William Hunt, "Why Did Orwell Go to Burma?" Orwell Society website, May 28, 2017, https://orwellsociety.com/why-did-orwell-go-to-burma/.

32 **"wintry conscience of a generation"**: V. S. Pritchett, "George Orwell," *New Statesman and Nation*, January 28, 1950, 96.

32 **"I hated the imperialism I was serving"**: *Road to Wigan Pier*, 126.

33 the otherwise unappealing character of Westfield: *Burmese Days* (New York: Harcourt, Brace, 1934), 74–75.

33 **"puny wisp of a man"**: "A Hanging," *Collected Essays*, vol. 1, 44–49.

34 **"place was on the other side"**: *Road to Wigan Pier*, 128.

36 **"crisp, fierce, and almost boisterous"**: Quoted in Crick, *A Life*, 265.

37 **"the whole of this second part"**: Victor Gollancz, foreword to *The Road to Wigan Pier* (New York: Harcourt, Brace, 1958 [1936]), xiv. (Note: This is the first US edition, which contains Gollancz's original Left Book Club foreword. Other citations refer to the Penguin edition.)

41 **"the war was worth winning"**: *Homage to Catalonia* (New York: Penguin Modern Classics, 2000 [1938]), 217.

41 *Animal Farm* and *Nineteen Eighty-Four* can be read: Emma Larkin, *Finding George Orwell in Burma* (New York: Penguin, 2006).

2. THE THOUGHT POLICE

43 **"If liberty means anything"**: "The Freedom of the Press," proposed preface to *Animal Farm*, first published in the *Times Literary Supplement*, September 15, 1972.

43 **"is the freedom to say"**: *Nineteen Eighty-Four* (New York: Signet Classic, 1971 [1949, 1961], with afterword by Erich Fromm), 81.

44 **"obviously . . . not desirable"**: "Freedom of the Press."

44 **"there is no freedom of speech"**: *The Road to Wigan Pier* (Harmondsworth, UK: Penguin, 1962 [1936]), 127.

44 **"If publishers and editors"**: "Freedom of the Press."

45 **"the real struggle in Spain"**: "Spilling the Spanish Beans," in *The Collected Essays, Journalism and Letters of George Orwell*, ed. Sonia Orwell and Ian Angus, vol. 1, *An Age Like This*, 273.

46 **"I do not agree"**: Letter to the editor of *Time and Tide*, February 5, 1938, in *Collected Essays*, vol. 1, 298.

46 **"It is a sort of charm"**: "As I Please," *Tribune*, June 9, 1944, in *The Collected Essays, Journalism and Letters of George Orwell*, ed. Sonia Orwell and Ian Angus, vol. 3, *As I Please* (New York: Harcourt, Brace, 1968), 169–70.

47 **"We are living Orwell's 1984"**: Donald J. Trump Jr. (@DonaldJTrumpJr), "We are living Orwell's 1984. Free-speech no longer exists in America. It died with big tech and what's left is only there for a chosen few. This is absolute insanity!" Twitter, January 8, 2021, 7:10 p.m., https://twitter.com/DonaldJTrumpJr/status/1347697226466828288.

48 **"This could not be more Orwellian"**: Josh Hawley (@HawleyMO), "My statement on the woke mob at @simonschuster," Twitter, January 7, 2021, 6:42 p.m., https://twitter.com/HawleyMO/status/1347327743004995585/photo/1.

48 **"This is a battle"**: Elon Musk (@elonmusk), "This is a battle for the future of civilization. If free speech is lost even in America, tyranny is all that lies ahead," Twitter, November 28, 2022, 8:41 p.m., https://twitter.com/elonmusk/status/1597405399040217088?lang=en.

49 **"Tech guru slams Twitter"**: Brian Flood and Nikolas Lanum, "Tech guru slams Twitter shadow banning as 'one step away from George Orwell's Thought Police,'" Fox News, December 12, 2022.

49 **"Even the White House"**: "Musk is fixing Twitter's censorship problem—no wonder the left is freaking out," *New York Post* editorial, November 30, 2022.

49 **"News outlets in particular"**: Gil Duran, "I just got myself banned from Elon Musk's Twitter. Here's why you should, too," *San Francisco Chronicle*, December 29, 2022.

50 **"Orwellian Grass/Cancel Culture"**: Paul Knaggs, "Cancel Culture: Two Minutes of Hate," *Labour Heartlands*, July 2, 2020.

51 **"it is not possible for us"**: Kingsley Martin, letter to Orwell, July 29, 1937, quoted in Bernard Crick, *George Orwell: A Life* (London: Secker & Warburg, 1980), 341.

52 **"The most important fact"**: "Review of the Spanish Cockpit," *Time and Tide*, July 31, 1937, in *Collected Essays*, vol. 1, 277–78.

52 **"never seemed to grasp the enormity"**: Crick, *A Life*, 342.

53 **"Decayed liberal. Very dishonest"**: Notebook entry, quoted in Christopher Hitchens, *Why Orwell Matters* (New York: Basic Books, 2002), 164.

54 **"?? Too dishonest to be outright 'crypto'"**: List of "crypto-communists, fellow-travellers or inclined that way," submitted to UK Information Research Department, May 2, 1949. Full list reprinted in *Guardian Review*, June 21, 2003.

54 **articles with lurid headlines:** Timothy Garton Ash, "Orwell's List," *New York Review of Books,* September 25, 2003.

54 **James Oliver and Paul Lashmar wrote:** Quoted in Hitchens, *Why Orwell Matters*, 155.

54 **Oliver went on to say:** Quoted in Hitchens, *Why Orwell Matters*, 156.

54 **As Celia Kirwan said to Ash:** Quoted in Ash, "Orwell's List."

55 **"Now, we are aware"**: "As I Please," *Tribune*, February 4, 1944, in *Collected Essays*, vol. 3, 88.

59 **what he termed "dying metaphors"**: "Politics and the English Language," *Horizon*, April 1946, in *The Collected Essays, Journalism and Letters of George Orwell*, ed. Sonia Orwell and Ian Angus, vol. 4, *In Front of Your Nose* (New York: Harcourt, Brace & World, 1968), 130.

59 **"Merriam-Webster declared *gaslighting*"**: "Word of the Year 2022," *Wordplay*, Merriam-Webster, accessed June 9, 2023, https://www.merriam -webster.com/words-at-play/word-of-the-year.

60 **"They can make you say"**: *Nineteen Eighty-Four*, 166.

60 **"Reality is inside the skull"**: *Nineteen Eighty-Four*, 265.

61 **motivated by "political purpose"**: "Why I Write," *Gangrel*, no. 4 (summer 1946), republished on the Orwell Foundation website, accessed June 9, 2023, https://www.orwellfoundation.com/the-orwell-foundation/orwell/ essays-and-other-works/why-i-write.

61 **"the passive voice"**: "Politics and the English Language," *Collected Essays*, vol. 4, 131.

62 **"What I have most wanted"**: "Why I Write."

63 **"the defence of the indefensible"**: This and the subsequent quotation in this section from "Politics and the English Language," *Collected Essays*, vol. 4, 136, 127–28.

65 **"B vocabulary" covered political language:** *Nineteen Eighty-Four*, 302ff.

65 **"ensure that appropriate conditions"**: "Universal Credit: Impact Assessment (IA)," Department for Work and Pensions, December 2012, accessed

June 9, 2023, https://assets.publishing.service.gov.uk/government/uploads
/system/uploads/attachment_data/file/220177/universal-credit-wr2011-ia
.pdf.

65 **"The purpose of Newspeak"**: *Nineteen Eighty-Four*, 303 and 313.

68 **"downright Orwellian"**: Chris Murphy (@ChrisMurphyCT), "It's getting
downright Orwellian in Florida. Big government tells you what books to
read. Big government tells teachers what they can say and can't say. Big
government punishes companies that dissent from the government line,"
Twitter, February 2, 2023, 9:43 a.m., https://twitter.com/ChrisMurphyCT/
status/1621157314119225345.

68 **"us[e] history teaching"**: Richard J. Evans, "Michael Gove's history wars,"
Guardian, July 13, 2013.

69 **"sociopathic, corrupt thug"**: Quoted in Hannah Furness, "Hay Festival
2013: Don't sign up to Gove's insulting curriculum, Schama urges," *Daily
Telegraph*, May 30, 2013.

69 **"That history [of Rhodes's imperialist atrocities]"**: Quoted in Aamna
Mohdin, "Protesters rally in Oxford for removal of Cecil Rhodes statue,"
Guardian, June 9, 2020.

70 **"Every record has been destroyed"**: "The statue-smashers are assaulting
democracy and civilization," *New York Post* editorial, June 27, 2020.

71 **"self-defined intersectional victims"**: Ruthie Blum, "The intersectionality
of antisemitism," *Jerusalem Post*, September 2, 2022.

71 **"to control minds by delving"**: Calvin Robinson, "As diversity lessons for
the civil service are scrapped, it's good riddance to the bunkum of 'unconscious race-bias' classes," *Daily Mail*, December 15, 2020.

71 **"These examples are misleading comparisons"**: Enzo Traverso, "Tear-
ing Down Statues Doesn't Erase History, It Makes Us See It More Clearly,"
Jacobin, June 24, 2020.

72 **"What could be more Orwellian"**: Priya Satia, "What's Really Orwellian
about Our Global Black Lives Matter Moment," *Slate*, June 30, 2020.

73 **scholars have used proxy data:** Haley McAvay and Gregory Verdugo,
"Income Inequality and Segregation in the Paris Metro Area (1990–
2015)," in *Urban Socio-Economic Segregation and Income Inequality: A Global Perspective*, ed. Maarten van Ham, Tiit Tammaru, Rūta
Ubarevičienė, and Heleen Janssen (Cham, Switzerland: Springer, 2021):
329–45.

73 **and on stops and arrests:** Rob Schmitz, "With far-right extremism on the
rise, Germany investigates its police," NPR, December 10, 2020.

73 **"I had reduced everything"**: *Road to Wigan Pier*, 129.

74 **"is NOT intended as an attack"**: Letter to Francis Henson, June 16, 1949,
in *Collected Essays*, vol. 4, 502.

3. ISMS

76 **"a boot stamping on a human face":** *Nineteen Eighty-Four*, with an after-word by Eric Fromm (New York: Penguin, 1984 [1949]), 267.

77 **"A nationalist is one who":** "Notes on Nationalism," in *The Collected Essays, Journalism and Letters of George Orwell*, ed. Sonia Orwell and Ian Angus, vol. 3, *As I Please* (New York: Harcourt, Brace, 1968), 363.

77 **a wide variety of toxic "nationalisms":** "Notes on Nationalism," in *Collected Essays*, vol. 3, 372–76.

78 **TASS news agency:** Kevin Liffey, "Orwell's novel of repression '1984' tops Russian bestseller lists," Reuters, December 13, 2022.

78 **online newspaper the *Moscow Times*:** "Moscow Times' Russian service blocked over war coverage," *Moscow Times*, April 15, 2022.

78 **"lawyer Anastasia Rudenko and":** "Explainer: How Orwell's '1984' looms large in wartime Russia," *Moscow Times*, May 26, 2022.

78 **Russia's foreign ministry claimed:** Pjotr Sauer, "Orwell's Nineteen Eighty-Four was about liberalism, not totalitarianism, claims Moscow diplomat," *Guardian*, May 23, 2022.

79 **"Orwell could not have dreamt":** Quoted in Liffey, "Orwell's novel of repression."

79 **"physical jerks":** *Nineteen Eighty-Four*, 31.

80 **"The greatest mistake is to imagine":** "As I Please," *Tribune*, June 9, 1944, in *Collected Essays*, vol. 3, 133.

81 **"incorporate education about a shared awareness":** Quoted in Chris Buckley, "Brushing off criticism, China's Xi calls policies in Xinjiang 'totally correct,'" *New York Times*, September 26, 2020.

82 **Sugarcandy Mountain, a mythical paradise:** *Animal Farm* (Harlow, UK: Heinemann, 1994 [1945]), 10.

82 **"hated Moses because":** *Animal Farm*, 10.

83 **"'No, sahib,' he would say":** *Burmese Days* (New York: Harcourt, Brace, 1934), 221.

83 **"a rat, a frog":** *Burmese Days*, 7.

83 **Gandhi "had lived just long enough":** "Reflections on Gandhi," in *The Collected Essays, Journalism and Letters of George Orwell*, ed. Sonia Orwell and Ian Angus, vol. 4, *In Front of Your Nose* (New York: Harcourt, Brace & World, 1968), 469–70.

84 **"hate Russian totalitarianism":** Letter to the Duchess of Atholl, November 15, 1945, in *Collected Essays*, vol. 4, 30.

84 **essay published in the *Adelphi*:** "Not Counting Niggers," in *The Collected Essays, Journalism and Letters of George Orwell*, ed. Sonia Orwell and Ian Angus, vol. 1, *An Age Like This* (New York: Harcourt, Brace & World, 1968), 394–98.

85 **"no modern man, in his heart of hearts":** *The Road to Wigan Pier* (Harmondsworth, UK: Penguin, 1962 [1936]), 126.

85 **"Foreign oppression," he claimed:** *Road to Wigan Pier*, 126.

85 **"One gets some idea of the real relationship":** "Not Counting Niggers," *Collected Essays*, vol. 1, 397.

86 **"the left-winger continues to feel":** *Road to Wigan Pier*, 140.

86 **"Under the capitalist system":** *Road to Wigan Pier*, 140.

87 **"a bottomless reserve of cheap labour":** *Nineteen Eighty-Four*, 187.

87 **"If it is really true":** *Tribune*, 1946, in *The Complete Works of George Orwell*, ed. Peter Davison, vol. 18 (London: Secker & Warburg, 1997), 142.

88 **According to the Census Bureau:** John Creamer, "Inequalities Persist Despite Decline in Poverty for All Major Race and Hispanic Origin Groups," US Census Bureau, September 15, 2020, https://www.census.gov/library/stories/2020/09/poverty-rates-for-blacks-and-hispanics-reached-historic-lows-in-2019.html.

88 **In the United Kingdom, data:** Jeena O'Neill, "Effects of Taxes and Benefits on UK Household Income: Financial Year Ending 2019," *Census 2021*, Office for National Statistics (UK), June 23, 2020, https://www.ons.gov.uk/peoplepopulationandcommunity/personalandhouseholdfinances/incomeandwealth/bulletins/theeffectsoftaxesandbenefitsonhouseholdincome/financialyearending2019.

89 **"The two great divisions of society":** Quoted in Ta-Nehisi Coates, "The Civil War Isn't Tragic, Cont.," *Atlantic*, April 26, 2011.

89 **"In an 'outpost of Empire'":** *Road to Wigan Pier*, 123–24.

89 **2019 AP-NORC poll:** Corey Williams and Noreen Nasir, "AP-NORC poll: Most Americans oppose reparations for slavery," Associated Press, October 25, 2019, https://apnews.com/article/va-state-wire-us-news-ap-top-news-slavery-mi-state-wire-76de76e9870b45d38390cc40e25e8f03.

90 **In 2013, CARICOM:** "About Us," CARICOM Reparations Commission, https://caricomreparations.org/about-us/.

90 **that France pay Haiti:** For a good discussion of this issue, see Constant Méheut, Catherine Porter, Selam Gebrekidan, and Matt Apuzzo, "The ransom: Demanding reparations, and ending up in exile," *New York Times*, May 20, 2022.

91 **Charles Blair, Orwell's great-great-grandfather:** For Blair and others' slave holdings, see the website maintained by the Centre for the Study of the Legacies of British Slavery at University College London's website, available at https://www.ucl.ac.uk/lbs/.

91 **"Do you realize that the past":** *Nineteen Eighty-Four*, 155.

92 **"are the victims of their condition":** Krishan Kumar, "Through a Burmese Lens: Class and Colonialism in the Works of George Orwell," *Times Literary Supplement*, November 25, 2022.

92 **"Shooting an Elephant":** "Shooting an Elephant," in *Collected Essays*, vol. 1, 235–42.

93 **"He was a Hindu":** "A Hanging," in *Collected Essays*, vol. 1, 44.

93 **The Asians in *Burmese Days*:** *Burmese Days*, 5 (for U Po Kyin); 36–37 (for Dr. Veraswami); 52 (for Ma Hla May). References to "seas" of Asians can be found on pages 102, 105, 246, and 251.

94 **recent book *Orwell and Empire*:** Douglas Kerr, *Orwell and Empire* (Oxford: Oxford University Press, 2022), 56 (for the Kerr quote); 4 (for the Gilroy quote).

94 **"managed both to love Englishness":** Rebecca Solnit, *Orwell's Roses* (London: Granta, 2021), 26. The Woolworth's quote appears on page 28.

95 **one of his wartime columns:** "As I Please," *Tribune*, January 21, 1944, in *Collected Essays*, vol. 3, 82.

95 **Orwell writes of patriotism:** "Notes on Nationalism," in *Collected Essays*, vol. 3, 362.

95 **"a faint feeling of sacrilege":** "My Country Right or Left," in *Collected Essays*, vol. 1, 540.

96 **"You have immediately":** Quoted in *The Orwell Reader: Fiction, Essays, and Reportage* (New York: Harvest Books, 1984 [1956]), 250.

96 **"a family in which the young":** Quoted in *Orwell Reader*, 261.

98 **"I was patriotic at heart":** "My Country Right or Left," in *Collected Essays*, vol. 1, 539.

4. INEQUALITY

101 **removal and replacement of the railings:** "As I Please," *Tribune*, August 4, 1944, in *The Collected Essays, Journalism and Letters of George Orwell*, ed. Sonia Orwell and Ian Angus, vol. 3, *As I Please* (New York: Harcourt, Brace, 1968), 200–201.

101 **"If giving the land of England back":** "As I Please," *Tribune*, August 18, 1944, in *Collected Essays*, vol. 3, 207.

102 **"the market economy and private property":** Thomas Piketty, *Time for Socialism: Dispatches from a World on Fire* (New Haven, CT: Yale University Press, 2021), 2.

103 **a *Wall Street Journal* review:** Daniel Shuchman, "Thomas Piketty revives Marx for the 21st century," *Wall Street Journal*, April 21, 2014.

103 **"League for the Dignity and Rights of Man":** Bernard Crick, *George Orwell: A Life* (London: Secker & Warburg, 1980), 497.

104 **"It was possible, no doubt":** *Nineteen Eighty-Four* (New York: Signet Classic, 1971 [1949, 1961], with afterword by Erich Fromm), 190.

105 **"the vast majority of people":** *Homage to Catalonia* (New York: Penguin Modern Classics, 2000 [1938]), 88.

106 **the pigs quietly amend the commandment:** *Animal Farm* (Harlow, UK: Heinemann, 1994 [1945]), 85.

106 **the wealthiest ten percent:** Thomas Piketty, *Capital in the Twenty-First Century* (Cambridge, MA: Harvard University Press, 2014), trans. Arthur Goldhammer, Fig. 10.3, 434.

107 **top two percent of taxpayers:** For historic income distributions, see Peter Scott and James T. Walker, "The Comfortable, the Rich, and the Super-Rich: What Really Happened to Top British Incomes during the First Half of the Twentieth Century?" *Journal of Economic History* 80, no. 1 (2020), 38–68.

108 **divided into three "castes":** "Such, Such Were the Joys," in *The Collected Essays, Journalism and Letters of George Orwell*, ed. Sonia Orwell and Ian Angus, vol. 4, *In Front of Your Nose* (New York: Harcourt, Brace & World, 1968), 339.

108 **"You were no good unless":** "Such, Such Were the Joys," in *Collected Essays*, vol. 4, 356.

108 **"Before [the First World War] the worship of money":** "Such, Such Were the Joys," in *Collected Essays*, vol. 4, 357.

109 **"intimately, intelligently snobbish" peers:** "Such, Such Were the Joys," in *Collected Essays*, vol. 4, 356.

109 **"far more *consciousness* of poverty":** *The Road to Wigan Pier* (Harmondsworth, UK: Penguin, 1962 [1936]), 108. Italics appear in the original text.

110 **"As parents increasingly believe":** Elizabeth Warren and Amelia Warren Tyagi, *The Two-Income Trap: Why Middle-Class Parents Are (Still) Going Broke* (New York: Basic Books, 2003), 33.

111 **In the Britain of 1911:** Derek Gillard, "1900–1923," chap. 7 in *Education in England: A History* (2018), www.educationengland.org.uk/history.

111 **Richard Reeves of the Brookings Institute:** Richard Reeves, "Stop pretending you're not rich," *New York Times*, June 10, 2017.

112 **"a family of 'poor whites'":** *Road to Wigan Pier*, 109.

112 **"really aware of the working class":** *Road to Wigan Pier*, 130.

114 **"He hated being the ruler":** V. S. Pritchett, script for a BBC broadcast on Orwell in the *Living Writers* series, to be broadcast on the Third Programme on November 23, 1946, at 11:30 p.m. Filed in Add. Ms. 73083, British Library, London.

116 **"You may have three halfpence":** *Road to Wigan Pier*, 79.

117 **"only tenpence a week on green vegetables":** *Road to Wigan Pier*, 85–86.

118 **"The peculiar evil is this":** *Road to Wigan Pier*, 86.

118 **Paltrow took up the challenge:** Lindsey Bever, "A hungry Gwyneth Paltrow fails the food-stamp challenge four days in," *Washington Post*, April 17, 2015.

119 **"I'm not judgmental, but"**: Alex Andreou, "Jamie Oliver, you haven't tasted real poverty. Cut out the tutting," *Guardian*, August 27, 2013.

120 **he related his ambivalence**: *Road to Wigan Pier*, 89–90.

121 **"When [my wife] Heidi's first lady"**: David Mack, "Cruz: When my wife is first lady 'french fries are coming back to the cafeteria,'" BuzzFeed News, January 31, 2016.

122 **the conservative *National Review* crowed**: Jonathan S. Tobin, "Chicago Repeals Its Soda Tax," *National Review*, October 17, 2017.

123 **In 2013, a working group**: Committee on Health Care for Underserved Women Breastfeeding Expert Work Group, "ACOG Committee Opinion 821," *Obstetrics & Gynecology* 137, no. 2 (February 2021), 54–62.

123 **"Even when I am on the verge"**: *Road to Wigan Pier*, 43.

123 **"I most certainly can blame him!"**: *A Clergyman's Daughter* (New York: Penguin Books 1990 [1935]), 25.

124 **forced into a "passive role"**: *Road to Wigan Pier*, 43.

124 **"people will put up with anything"**: *Road to Wigan Pier*, 46.

125 **"'Fixing it' often meant**: Matthew Desmond, *Evicted: Poverty and Profit in the American City* (New York: Broadway Books, 2016), 72.

126 **"If there was hope"**: *Nineteen Eighty-Four*, 220.

5. PATRIARCHY

130 **"every fruit-juice drinker"**: *The Road to Wigan Pier* (Harmondsworth, UK: Penguin, 1962 [1936]), 152.

131 **"suspected that the war between the sexes"**: Christopher Hitchens, *Why Orwell Matters* (New York: Basic Books, 2002), 154.

132 **Beddoe's critique of Orwell**: Deidre Beddoe, "Hindrances and Help-Meets: Women in the Writings of George Orwell," in *Orwell: Views from the Left*, ed. Christopher Norris (London: Lawrence & Wishart, 1984), 140.

133 **"a rebel from the waist down"**: *Nineteen Eighty-Four* (New York: Signet Classic, 1971 [1949, 1961], with afterword by Erich Fromm), 156.

134 **Planned Parenthood classifies**: "Roe v. Wade Overturned: How the Supreme Court Let Politicians Outlaw Abortion," Planned Parenthood website.

134 **President Joe Biden characterized *Roe***: "Remarks by President Biden on the Supreme Court Decision to Overturn Roe v. Wade," White House Briefing Room, June 24, 2022, 12:37 p.m. EDT, https://www.whitehouse.gov/briefing-room/speeches-remarks/2022/06/24/remarks-by-president-biden-on-the-supreme-court-decision-to-overturn-roe-v-wade/.

136 **"Gordon had a sort of secret feud"**: *Keep the Aspidistra Flying* (London: Penguin, 2000 [1936]), 29.

136 **"Rosemary, his girl, who loved him"**: *Aspidistra*, 14.

137 **"take your chance"**: *Aspidistra*, 157.

137 **"We shall have to get married"**: *Aspidistra*, 252.

137 **Rosemary doesn't want to be pregnant**: *Aspidistra*, 251, 253.

138 **" 'No fear!' he said"**: *Aspidistra*, 253, 255.

138 **A 1937 UK government report**: Ministry of Health, *Report of an Investigation into Maternal Mortality*, Cmd. 5422 (London: His Majesty's Stationery Office, 1937).

139 **A 2009 article**: Iqbal Shah and Elisabeth Ahman, "Unsafe Abortion: Global and Regional Incidence, Trends, Consequences and Challenges," *Journal of Obstetrics and Gynaecology Canada* 31, no. 12 (December 2009), 1149–58.

139 **"Abortion must be the key"**: Quoted in Stephen Brooke, *Sexual Politics: Sexuality, Family Planning, and the British Left from the 1880s to the Present Day* (Oxford: Oxford University Press, 2011), 102.

140 **Stella Browne proclaimed herself**: Lesley Hall, *The Life and Times of Stella Browne: Feminist and Free Spirit* (London: I. B. Tauris, 2011), 21.

140 **"some kind of Aldous Huxley *Brave New World*"**: *Aspidistra*, 97.

141 **"It gave him a shock to see it"**: *Aspidistra*, 260.

141 **"His baby had seemed real to him"**: *Aspidistra*, 261.

142 **a piece in *Newsweek* magazine**: Ingrid Skop and Mary Szoch, "Abortion Advocates are Resorting to Orwellian Language Game," *Newsweek*, March 22, 2022.

143 **call him a "Tory radical"**: See John Rodden, "George Orwell, Pickwickian Radical? An Ambivalent Case," *Kenyon Review* 12, no. 3 (1990): 139–49; Peter Wilkin, "George Orwell: The English Dissident as Tory Anarchist," *Political Studies* 61, no. 1 (2013), 197–214.

143 **"if you are not willing"**: John Fetterman, "Protecting Women's Reproductive Freedom," 2022 US Senate campaign statement, https://johnfetterman.com/issue/protecting-womens-reproductive-freedom/.

144 **a "secondary contradiction"**: Laura Beers, "The Secondary Contradiction of Women of the Radical Left," *Journal of Women's History* 31, no. 3 (2019), 129–35.

146 **"challenging issues related to violence"**: Chris Hastings, "Wokery beyond parody because university slaps a TRIGGER warning on George Orwell's 1984 as it contains 'explicit material' which some students may find 'offensive and upsetting,' " *Daily Mail*, January 22, 2022.

146 **"Vivid, beautiful hallucinations"**: *Nineteen Eighty-Four*, 15.

147 **" 'I hated the sight of you' "**: *Nineteen Eighty-Four*, 121.

147 **"Charlie, one of the local curiosities"**: *Down and Out in Paris and London* (London: Victor Gollancz, 1933), 12–19.

149 **a *Tribune* review of the book's**: Daniel George, *Tribune*, January 24, 1941, 13.

149 **"Where," she laments:** Daphne Patai, *The Orwell Mystique: A Study in Male Ideology* (Amherst, MA: University of Massachusetts Press, 1984), 16.

150 **Kerr suggests that the scene:** Douglas Kerr, *Orwell and Empire* (Oxford: Oxford University Press, 2022), 98.

150 **"had bought . . . from her parents":** *Burmese Days* (New York: Harcourt, Brace, 1934), 53.

150 **"Get out of this room!":** *Burmese Days*, 55.

151 **He describes her, variously:** *Burmese Days*, 53, 155.

151 **"at least be like the animals":** *Aspidistra*, 113.

151 **"tried to rape Dorothy":** Quoted in *A Kind of Compulsion (Complete Orwell)*, ed. Peter Davison (London: Secker & Warburg, 2000), 361.

151 **the published version ultimately ran:** *A Clergyman's Daughter* (New York: Penguin Books 1990 [1935]), 87.

152 **"Of course in practice one never does":** *Coming Up for Air* (New York: Harcourt, Brace, 1950 [1939]), 158–59.

153 **"During the first few weeks":** Quoted in Sylvia Topp, *Eileen: The Making of George Orwell* (London: Unbound, 2020), 138.

153 **Bowling recalls his first girlfriend:** *Coming Up for Air*, 121.

155 **"tells me that my anti-feminist views":** Letter to Brenda Salkeld, July 27, 1934, in *The Collected Essays, Journalism and Letters of George Orwell*, ed. Sonia Orwell and Ian Angus, vol. 1, *An Age Like This* (New York: Harcourt, Brace & World, 1968), 136.

155 **"He didn't really like women":** Quoted in Hitchens, *Why Orwell Matters*, 144.

155 **"wished I could sleep with you":** Quoted in Topp, *Eileen*, 294.

156 **In the postscript, Venables claimed:** Dione Venables, postscript to Jacintha Buddicom, *Eric and Us: The Postscript Edition* (London: Finlay, 2006).

157 **He casually refers to the assault:** Gordon Bowker, "Blair Pounces," *Times Literary Supplement* no. 5421, February 23, 2007, 15.

157 **"the attempted 'rape' ":** Kathryn Hughes, "Such were the joys," *Guardian*, February 17, 2007.

157 **Thus, John Sutherland's *Orwell's Nose*:** John Sutherland, *Orwell's Nose: A Pathological Biography* (London: Reaktion Books, 2016), 87.

158 **Orwell's "dirty old man" perversions:** Craig Brown, "Was Orwell just a dirty old man?" *Daily Mail*, February 14, 2018.

6. BLUEPRINT FOR REVOLUTION

162 **"Mr. Orwell does not once":** Victor Gollancz, foreword to *The Road to Wigan Pier* (New York: Harcourt, Brace, 1958 [1936]), xxii–xxiii. (Note: This is the first US edition, which contains Gollancz's original Left Book Club foreword. Other citations refer to the Penguin edition.)

162 **Orwell did clearly articulate:** *The Lion and the Unicorn* (London: Secker & Warburg, 1941), 96.

163 **Orwell was an uneasy admixture:** Peter Stansky, *The Socialist Patriot: George Orwell and War* (Stanford, CA: Stanford University Press, 2023), 74.

163 **"to be a Socialist, though Tory":** Eileen Blair letter to Norah Miles, December 1940, in *George Orwell: A Life in Letters*, ed. Peter Davison (London: Penguin, 2011), 184.

164 **"everyone called everyone else 'Comrade'":** *Homage to Catalonia* (New York: Penguin Modern Classics, 2000 [1938]), 3.

164 **"vitally necessary to do something":** Quoted in Stansky, *Socialist Patriot*, 69.

164 **"the highest tax-free income":** *Lion and the Unicorn*, 99.

164 **"the underlying fact":** *Lion and the Unicorn*, 37.

165 **"nationalization of land":** *Lion and the Unicorn*, 99.

165 **excepting the temporary wartime nationalization:** For a contemporary discussion on nationalization in Britain during World War I, see Arthur Greenwood, "The Nationalization Movement in Great Britain," *Atlantic*, March 1920. For French nationalization in the run-up to World War II, see Jeffrey Clarke, "The Nationalization of War Industries in France, 1936–1937: A Case Study," *Journal of Modern History* 49, no. 3 (1977), 411–30.

165 **"changes that will surprise the idiots":** "My Country, Right or Left," in *The Collected Essays, Journalism and Letters of George Orwell*, ed. Sonia Orwell and Ian Angus, vol. 1, *An Age Like This* (New York: Harcourt, Brace & World, 1968), 539.

165 **"When the real English Socialist movement":** "Socialism and Democracy," in *The Betrayal of the Left: An Examination and Refutation of Communist Policy from October 1939 to January 1941*, ed. Victor Gollancz (London: Victor Gollancz, 1941).

166 **"an all-important English trait":** *Lion and the Unicorn*, 22.

167 **"The railway shareholders":** "London Letter," *Partisan Review*, summer 1946, in *The Collected Essays, Journalism and Letters of George Orwell*, ed. Sonia Orwell and Ian Angus, vol. 4, *In Front of Your Nose* (New York: Harcourt, Brace & World, 1968), 186.

168 **Jose Harris and Steven Fielding:** Jose Harris, "War and Social History: Britain and the Home Front during the Second World War," *Contemporary European History* 1, no. 1 (1992), 17–35; Steven Fielding, "The spirit of the Blitz isn't back, it's bunk," *Financial Times*, March 19, 2020.

169 **"Our generation has never been tested":** Matt Hancock, "We must all do everything in our power to protect lives," *Financial Times*, March 14, 2020.

169 **"In these uncertain times":** Dave Laing, "Dame Vera Lynn obituary," *Guardian*, June 18, 2020.

169 **"We must act as in wartime":** Quoted in Fielding, "Spirit of the Blitz."

169 **"Now it's our time":** Quoted in Jeff Greenfield, "No, the Covid Fight Isn't Like WWII—and That's Bad News," *Politico,* May 9, 2020.

169 **Emmanuel Macron used the language of war:** Michael Rose and Richard Lough, "'We are at war': France imposes lockdown to combat virus," Reuters, March 16, 2020.

169 **"since German unification":** "Merkel calls coronavirus biggest challenge since WWII," Deutsche Welle website, March 18, 2020.

171 **"chasmic, impassable" barrier:** *The Road to Wigan Pier* (Harmondsworth, UK: Penguin, 1962 [1936]), 113.

171 **"a training in class prejudice":** *Lion and the Unicorn,* 104.

171 **"In the social set-up":** "London Letter," *Partisan Review,* summer 1946, *Collected Essays,* vol. 4, 186.

172 **over sixty percent of the ministers:** Ben Walker, "Sunak's Cabinet is overwhelmingly private school educated," *New Statesman,* October 26, 2022 (data from the Sutton Trust).

173 **nearly three-hundred-fold:** Paul Bolton, "Higher Education Student Numbers," *Commons Library Research Briefing,* February 21, 2023, 32.

174 **"a difficult question":** Letter to Julian Symonds, October 29, 1948, in *Collected Essays,* vol. 4, 451.

175 **Several studies conducted:** "Education in a Pandemic: The Disparate Impacts of COVID-19 on America's Students," US Department of Education, Office for Civil Rights, June 2021, published online at https://www2 .ed.gov/about/offices/list/ocr/docs/20210608-impacts-of-covid19.pdf; Emma Howard, Aneesa Khan, and Charlotte Lockyer, "Learning During the Pandemic: Review of Research from England," Office of Qualifications and Examinations Regulation (Ofqual), July 12, 2021, https://www .gov.uk/government/publications/learning-during-the-pandemic/learning -during-the-pandemic-review-of-research-from-england#the-differential -experiences-of-learning-loss.

178 **Biden has announced his commitment:** Lindsay Wagner, "Biden-Harris Administration Wants to Provide Free School Meals for All Students," EducationNC website, September 30, 2022, https://www.ednc.org/biden-harris -administration-wants-to-provide-free-school-meals-for-all-students/.

179 **he purported that royal sentiment:** "London Letter," *Partisan Review,* January 15, 1944, in *The Collected Essays, Journalism and Letters of George Orwell,* ed. Sonia Orwell and Ian Angus, vol. 3, *As I Please* (New York: Harcourt, Brace, 1968), 80–81.

180 **"immediate Dominion status":** *Lion and the Unicorn,* 99.

180 **"some kind of trade agreement":** Letter to Tom Wintringham, August 17, 1942. Add. Ms. 73083, British Library, London.

181 **"My friend, it iss pathetic":** *Burmese Days* (New York: Harcourt, Brace, 1934), 40.

182 **independence "would be a disaster":** *Lion and the Unicorn*, 105.

182 **total value of wealth drained:** Jason Hickel, "How Britain stole $45 trillion from India," Al Jazeera, December 19, 2018.

183 **Donald Trump similarly scaled:** Rob Garver, "Biden budget substantially boosts foreign aid, diplomacy, but raises defense by 1.7%," Voice of America, May 28, 2021; "Fiscal Year (FY) 2024 President's Budget Request for the United States Agency for International Development (USAID)," United States Agency for International Development, March 2023, https://www .usaid.gov/sites/default/files/2023-03/USAID_FY2024_BudgetRequest_ FactSheet3a.pdf.

183 **"I hope we never find life":** Donald Trump, @realDonaldTrump, Twitter, June 4, 2014, 9:59 a.m., https://twitter.com/realDonaldTrump/status/ 474188805541748736.

184 **"coloured peoples" of the British Empire:** *Lion and the Unicorn*, 99.

184 **"at present, rich countries":** Tedros Adhanom Ghebreyesus, "Vaccine Nationalism Harms Everyone and Protects No One," *Foreign Policy*, February 2, 2021.

185 **doses the US had shipped:** "Inequality of Pandemic Proportions: State and Pharma Failures not to be be Repeated," Amnesty International, March 2023. For up-to-date figures on domestic US and international COVID vaccine deliveries, see the Centers for Disease Control and Prevention COVID data tracker (https://covid.cdc.gov/covid-data-tracker/#vaccinations_vacc -total-admin-rate-total), or the US Department of State COVID-19 vaccine donations tracker (https://www.state.gov/covid-19-recovery/vaccine -deliveries/).

186 **"If and when she is replaced":** Sylvia Topp, *Eileen: The Making of George Orwell* (London: Unbound, 2020), 282.

188 **According to UN data:** Ashley Stahl, "The Pandemic and the Gender Pay Gap in 2022," *Forbes*, January 21, 2022.

189 **a significant role in Labour's landslide:** Books such as Paul Addison's *The Road to 1945: British Politics and the Second World War* (London: Jonathan Cape, 1975) and Angus Calder's *The People's War* (London: Pantheon, 1969) drew a direct line from the emergence of the "Blitz spirit" to the 1945 Labour victory and the birth of the welfare state. Research by myself (*Your Britain: Media and the Making of the Labour Party* [Cambridge, MA: Harvard University Press, 2010]) and others has since sought to nuance this argument.

AFTERWORD: FOR FREEDOM'S SAKE

192 **in part to a "historical impulse":** "Why I Write," *Gangrel*, no. 4 (summer 1946), available at https://www.orwellfoundation.com/the-orwell -foundation/orwell/essays-and-other-works/why-i-write/.

195 **"I do not believe"**: Letter to Francis A. Henson, June 16, 1949, *The Collected Essays, Journalism and Letters of George Orwell*, ed. Sonia Orwell and Ian Angus, vol. 4, *In Front of Your Nose* (New York: Harcourt, Brace & World, 1968), 502.

195 **"wintry conscience of a generation"**: V. S. Pritchett, "George Orwell," *New Statesman and Nation*, January 28, 1950, 96.

196 **"a writer of acute and penetrating temper"**: *Times* (London, UK), January 25, 1950, 7.

196 **"his uncompromising intellectual honesty"**: Arthur Koestler, "A rebel's progress," *Observer*, January 29, 1950, 4.

196 **"intellectual Socialist who preached"**: "Obituary: George Orwell," *Manchester Guardian*, January 23, 1950, 5.

197 **"Two Novels Popular Here"**: "George Orwell, author, 46, dead," *New York Times*, January 22, 1950, 77.

197 **"to remind us that we have never read Marx"**: Eileen Blair letter to Norah Myles, in *George Orwell: A Life in Letters*, ed. Peter Davison (London: Penguin, 2011), 95.

199 **"We present our society as being"**: Eric Fromm, afterword to *Nineteen Eighty-Four* (New York: Signet Classic, 1971 [1949, 1961]), 324.

199 **"Many critics view"**: Edwin McDowell, "'Nineteen Eighty-Four' is best seller again," *New York Times*, January 18, 1984, A1.

202 **"Apparently nothing will ever teach"**: Joe Pinsker, "What Can Explain the Success of Piketty's Capital?" *Atlantic*, September 23, 2014.

202 hostility to government was **"simply irrational"**: Francis Fukuyama, *Liberalism and Its Discontents* (London: Profile Books, 2022).

203 **"great numbers of well-to-do bourgeois"**: *Homage to Catalonia* (New York: Penguin Modern Classics, 2000 [1938]), 4.

203 **Bozo the scrivener**: *Down and Out in Paris and London* (London: Victor Gollancz, 1933), 218–27.

203 **"It is curious," Orwell remarks**: "A Hanging," in *Collected Essays*, in *The Collected Essays, Journalism and Letters of George Orwell*, ed. Sonia Orwell and Ian Angus, vol. 1, *An Age Like This* (New York: Harcourt, Brace & World, 1968), 45.

204 **"The mystical reverence that he felt"**: *Nineteen Eighty-Four* (New York: Signet Classic, 1971 [1949, 1961]), 219–20.

205 **the farm animals' anthem**: *Animal Farm* (Harlow, UK: Heinemann, 1994 [1945]), 7.

INDEX

Abbott, Diane, 174
abortion, 133–44
  backroom, 138–39
  as civil rights issue, 139–40
  feminist views of, 133–34, 139, 153, 199
  invocations of Orwell and, 142, 199
  legalization of, 133
  Orwell's androcentrism and, 132–33, 134–38, 140, 141–42
  Orwell's secular humanism and, 141
  political conflicts over, 133–34, 139–40, 142–44
  progressive ambivalence on, 142–44
  socialism and, 140–41
Abortion Law Reform Association (Britain), 134, 139
Adam, Eugene, 34
After Empire (Gilroy), 94
Allen, Woody, 159
alternative facts, 56
American Rescue Plan, 178
Andreou, Alex, 119–20
Animal Farm (Orwell)
  androcentrism in, 135
  censorship and, 47, 57–58
  Cold War and, 75
  cynicism in, 161
  Eastern European publication, 198
  on imperialism, 13
  popularity of, 16, 47
  religion in, 82
  Spanish Civil War and, 40, 41

Stalinism and, 13, 41, 103, 106, 194
  US reputation and, 196
antisemitism, 50–51, 81
Aristide, Jean-Bertrand, 90
Ash, Timothy Garton, 54
Atholl, Duchess of, 84
Attlee, Clement, 13, 53, 54, 74, 166, 171–72, 179, 187
authoritarianism
  China, 80–81, 193, 199
  corporate power and, 193
  current resurgence of, 17–18
  monarchy and, 179
  Orwell's opposition to, 13, 16
  working-class apathy and, 126
  See also fascism; Stalinism; totalitarianism

Barnes, Djuna, 154
Beddoe, Deidre, 132
Behr, Rafael, 12
Bevan, Anuerin "Nye," 194
Biden, Joe
  abortion and, 134, 143
  class and, 112
  democratic fragility and, 17
  economic inequality and, 177, 178
  imperial power debts and, 183
  invocations of Orwell and, 11
Black Curriculum campaign (Britain), 69, 91
Black Lives Matter movement, 69, 70–73, 91

Blair, Avril (Orwell's sister), 26, 35, 143, 187

Blair, Charles (Orwell's great-great-grandfather), 24, 91

Blair, Eileen O'Shaughnessy (Orwell's wife)
  class and, 24
  death of, 53
  diet of, 118, 122
  education of, 173
  "End of the Century, 1984," 80n
  marital conflict and, 153
  on Marx, 196–97
  Orwell's androcentrism and, 155
  on Orwell's patriotism, 163
  patriarchy and, 186, 187
  Spanish Civil War and, 39, 45

Blair, Eric. See Orwell, George

Blair, Ida Limouzin (Orwell's mother), 24–25, 26

Blair, Marjorie (Orwell's sister), 25

Blair, Richard (Dick) Walmesley (Orwell's father), 23, 25–26

Blair, Richard (Orwell's son), 29, 174, 187

Blair, Tony, 100, 104–5, 144, 157, 172–73, 179

Blum, Ruthie, 71

Bolsonaro, Jair, 12

book bans, 67–68

Borkenau, Franz, 51–52

Bowker, Gordon, 157

breastfeeding, 122–23

Brief History of Equality, A (Piketty), 201

Britain's Secret Propaganda War (Oliver and Lashmar), 54

British empire. See imperialism

British left
  on economic inequality, 104
  feminism and, 129, 130–31, 144
  imperialism and, 86
  Information Research Department list and, 54
  Orwell's alienation from, 196
  Orwell's criticisms of, 37–38, 86, 129–30
  patriotism and, 95, 96
  Spanish Civil War and, 46, 58
  support for Soviet Union, 46, 53, 64, 194

Brooke, Stephen, 134

Brown, Craig, 158–59

Brown, Des, 144

Brown, Gordon, 172–73

Browne, Stella, 139, 140

Buddicom, Jacintha, 26, 28, 30–31, 155–56, 157

Buddicom, Prosper, 26, 155

Burke, Edmund, 163

Burmese Days (Orwell)
  anti-imperialism in, 32–33, 36, 41, 182
  on censorship, 44
  Orwell's US reputation and, 196
  publication of, 36
  racism and, 92, 93–94, 181
  on religion, 82–83
  sexual predation in, 150–51
  tragedy in, 135
  on "white man's burden," 181

Calhoun, John C., 89, 90

Campbell, Beatrix, 126, 132

"cancel culture," 11, 44, 47–51, 57, 158–59, 200–201
  See also invocations of Orwell

Capital in the Twenty-First Century (Piketty), 100–101, 103, 201–2

capitalism
  advertising and, 200
  authoritarian resurgence and, 17–18
  benefits of, 115
  economic inequality and, 167–68

neoliberalism, 202, 203
Orwell's blueprint for socialist
    revolution and, 162
Capitol insurrection (Jan. 6, 2021), 11,
    47–48, 76
Carlson, Tucker, 95
Catholicism, 81, 143, 144
censorship
    "cancel culture" as, 47–51, 57,
        200–201
    gaslighting and, 58–59
    imperialism and, 44
    Nineteen Eighty-Four on, 47, 52, 57
    of Orwell's works, 44–47, 51–52,
        57–59
    truth and, 55, 56–57
    See also intellectual silencing
Charles III (king of England), 179
China, 80–81, 193, 199
Churchill, Winston, 30, 186, 202
Clash (Wilkinson), 153
class
    apathy and, 125–26
    cognitive dissonance and, 111–12
    credit and, 123–24
    current economic conditions and,
        99–101
    diet and, 116–23
    education and, 110–11
    escapism and, 115–16
    housing and, 124–25
    Orwell's blueprint for socialist revo-
        lution and, 163–64, 171
    Orwell's Burma IPS service and, 29,
        112–13
    Orwell's family background and, 24,
        28, 29, 107–8, 109–10, 114
    Orwell's London and Paris sojourns
        and, 35, 113–14
    private property and, 101–2
    The Road to Wigan Pier on, 28,
        114–15, 116–18, 120, 171

    social stratification and, 106–7,
        163–64
    See also economic inequality
Clergyman's Daughter, A (Orwell), 36,
    123–24, 151–52
climate change, 191
Clinton, Bill, 100, 104–5, 156–57
Coates, Ta-Nehisi, 89
Colbert, Jean-Baptiste, 70
Cold War
    disinformation and, 53
    doublethink and, 199
    end of, 156, 199–200
    Nineteen Eighty-Four and, 41, 75
    Orwell's blueprint for socialist
        revolution and, 189–90
    Orwell's Information Research
        Department list and, 51, 52–55
    popular understandings of Orwell
        and, 75–76, 198
Collings, Dennis, 35
Colston, Edward, 69
Coming Up for Air (Orwell), 25,
    36–37, 135, 152–53
Common, Jack, 29
Confederate statues, 70
Connolly, Cyril, 27, 30, 36
Conway, Kellyanne, 56
Cooperative movement (Britain), 134
Corbyn, Jeremy, 50, 57
COVID-19 pandemic, 168–71,
    175–78, 184–85, 188
Crick, Bernard, 51
Cripps, Stafford, 180
Cruz, Ted, 121
curriculum conflicts, 66–67, 68–69,
    71, 91
Curtis, Richard, 99

Darkness at Noon (Koestler), 103
Davies, Geraint, 131
Debs, Eugene V., 109

democracy, current threats to, 17–18,
    193
Democratic Party (United States), 104,
    131, 143, 156–57
DeSantis, Ron, 67
Desmond, Matthew, 124–25, 201
diet, 116–23
disinformation
    Cold War and, 53
    invocations of Orwell and, 11, 200
    Orwell's critique of, 16, 40, 61
    World War II and, 55–56
*Dobbs v. Jackson Women's Health
    Organization,* 133–34, 142–43
"Don't Say Gay" law (Florida, 2022),
    66–67
doublethink, 112, 198–99
Down and Out in Paris and London
    (Orwell), 34–35
    common humanity in, 203
    limitations of, 113–14
    Orwell's pen name and, 23, 34
    Orwell's social awakening and, 35
    Orwell's US reputation and, 196
    publication of, 35–36
    sexual predation in, 147–50, 151, 152
Duran, Gil, 49, 51

economic inequality
    COVID-19 pandemic and, 170–71,
        175–78
    current increase in, 99–101, 102,
        104–5, 107, 110–11, 193
    education and, 171–75
    invocations of Orwell and, 202
    nutrition and, 176–77, 178
    Orwell's blueprint for socialist
        revolution and, 164–65, 166–68,
        201–2
    patriarchy and, 166–67
    postwar alleviation of, 166–67
    racism and, 88–89

    social capital and, 106–7
    socialism and, 102–3, 104
    See also class
education
    book bans, 67–68
    class and, 110–11
    COVID-19 pandemic and, 175–76
    curriculum conflicts, 66–67, 68–69,
        71, 91
    inequality in, 171–75
    nutrition and, 176–77, 178
    Orwell's background, 25–30, 107–8,
        111
Eliot, T. S., 57–58
"End of the Century, 1984" (Blair), 80*n*
enslavement, 24, 89–91, 167
Eric & Us (Buddicom), 155–56
euphemism. *See* obfuscation
Evans, Richard, 68
Evicted (Desmond), 124–25
"Eyewitness in Spain" (Orwell), 51

"fake news" accusations, 11
Family Research Council (United
    States), 142
Fane, Mary (Orwell's great-great-
    grandmother), 24
fascism
    antisemitism and, 51
    Nineteen Eighty-Four on, 76
    Orwell's opposition to, 12, 38, 184
    quietism and, 36–37
    religion and, 81
    Spanish Civil War and, 38, 39, 45
fashion, 88, 115, 116
feminism
    on abortion, 133–34, 139, 153, 199
    British left and, 129, 130–31, 144
    interwar, 130–31, 139, 153–54
    on Orwell's androcentrism, 132
    See also patriarchy
Fetterman, John, 143

Fielding, Steven, 168
Fierz, Mabel, 35
food deserts, 122
Four Weddings and a Funeral, 99
Franco, Francisco, 38, 41, 45
"Freedom of the Press, The" (Orwell),
    44
free speech
    Animal Farm on, 75
    devaluation of, 74
    socialism and, 193
    vs. truth, 43–44, 51, 55–57, 62
Fromm, Erich, 198–99
Fukuyama, Francis, 202
Funder, Anna, 158

Gandhi, Mohandas, 83
Gas Light (Hamilton), 58
gaslighting, 58, 59–60
Geismer, Lily, 104
gender inequality. *See* patriarchy
George V (king of England), 179
Ghebreyesus, Tedros Adhanom,
    184–85
Gilroy, Paul, 94
Ginsburg, Ruth Bader, 139–40
Global South. *See* imperialism
Gollancz, Victor
    on common humanity, 204
    Down and Out in Paris and London
        and, 35–36
    economic inequality and, 103
    Homage to Catalonia and, 44–46,
        58–59
    Orwell's androcentrism and, 151–52
    on Orwell's blueprint for socialist
        revolution, 162
    The Road to Wigan Pier and, 37–38,
        124
Gopnik, Adam, 12
Gorbachev, Mikhail, 199
Gorsuch, Neil, 11–12

Gove, Michael, 68–69
Gow, Andrew, 30
Grant, Hugh, 99
Great Depression, 37
Great Recession (2008), 100, 105, 202

Haiti, 90
Hamilton, Patrick, 58
Hancock, Matt, 169
"Hanging, A" (Orwell), 33, 92, 93, 203–4
Hardie, Keir, 109
Harris, Jose, 168
Hawley, Josh, 11, 48, 51, 57, 75–76
Hayek, Friedrich, 190
Hemings, Sally, 159
"History Wars" (Britain), 68–69, 91
Hitchens, Christopher, 53, 54, 131, 200
Hitler, Adolf, 39
"Hollywood Ten," 55
Holtby, Winifred, 153–54
Homage to Catalonia (Orwell)
    Eileen Blair in, 39
    censorship and, 44–47, 52, 57,
        58–59
    on class, 164
    public exposure to, 18
    on Stalinism, 40–41, 45, 76
    US reputation and, 196
House of Lords, 179
House Un-American Activities Com-
    mittee (HUAC), 55
"How the Poor Die" (Orwell), 34
Hughes, Kathryn, 157
Hurston, Zora Neale, 154

imperialism
    censorship and, 44
    compensation to enslavers and, 24,
        89–91, 167
    curriculum conflicts and, 68–69, 91
    decolonization, 180–81, 183–84, 191
    ethnic/religious conflicts and, 83

imperialism (*continued*)
  Orwell's Burma IPS service and, 30,
    31–34, 84
  Orwell's family and, 23–26
  persistence of, 88–89
  reparations for, 90–91, 182–83,
    184–85
  statue removal campaigns and,
    69–70
  Ukraine war and, 97–98
  "white man's burden" and, 181, 182
  See also Orwell's anti-imperialism
Independent Labour Party (Britain),
  109
India. *See* imperialism
Indo-Pakistani War (1947–48), 83
"Inside the Whale" (Orwell), 37, 53, 162
intellectual silencing, 65–69
International Workers of the World
  (IWW), 109
internet, 190, 200–201
invocations of Orwell, 11–12
  abortion and, 142, 199
  antisemitism and, 50–51
  Black Lives Matter movement and,
    71–73
  "cancel culture" and, 47–50, 51
  Capitol insurrection and, 11, 47–48,
    76
  China and, 200
  critiques of, 71–73
  curriculum conflicts and, 71
  economic inequality and, 202
  internet and, 200–201
  Orwell as cultural product and, 16
  statue removal campaigns and, 70
  truth vs. free speech and, 57

Jackson, Lydia, 157–58
Jaques, Eleanor, 35
Jefferson, Thomas, 159
Johnson, Boris, 12, 168, 169, 183

Keep the Aspidistra Flying (Orwell),
  36, 134–38, 140, 141–42,
  151
Kelly, Ruth, 144
Kerr, Douglas, 94, 150
Khan, Sadiq, 178
Kipling, Rudyard, 181
Kirwan, Celia, 53, 54
Koestler, Arthur, 103, 196
Kumar, Krishan, 92

Labour Heartlands, 50, 51
Labour Party (Britain)
  abortion and, 134, 144, 153
  "cancel culture" and, 50–51, 57
  capitalism and, 167–68
  Cold War and, 53
  decolonization and, 180–81
  educational inequality and, 171–73,
    174
  imperialism and, 86
  Information Research Department
    list, 51, 52–55
  Orwell's support for, 13, 74, 163,
    196
  patriarchy and, 131, 187
  Popular Front and, 46
  socialism and, 74
  See also British left
language
  doublethink, 112, 198–99
  intellectual silencing and, 65–69
  obfuscation in, 63–65, 66, 80–81
  propaganda, 16
  quality of, 61–63
  See also truth
Lashmar, Paul, 54
League for European Freedom, 84
Lee, Robert E., 70
Left Behind (Geismer), 104
Left Book Club (LBC), 37, 46
LGBTQ oppression, 66–67, 68

Liberalism and Its Discontents (Fuku-
    yama), 202
Life (Britain), 142
Limouzin, Frank, 25
Limouzin, G. E., 24
Limouzin, Nellie (Orwell's aunt), 34
Lion and the Unicorn, The (Orwell),
    13, 96–97, 162, 166, 179, 180,
    182, 204
London, Jack, 114
Ludlow, John Malcolm, 109
Lynn, Vera, 169

Macron, Emmanuel, 169, 170
MAGA movement, 90
Martin, Kingsley, 51–52, 53–54, 58–59
Marx, Karl, 196–97
media, 115–16
Merkel, Angela, 169–70
#MeToo movement, 59, 133, 155
Miller, Henry, 37
Miller, J. Howard, 185–86
Milosz, Czesław, 198
Murphy, Chris, 68
Murphy, Paul, 144
Musk, Elon, 48–49
Mussolini, Benito, 38, 39
"My Country Right or Left" (Orwell),
    29, 165

National Association to Repeal Abor-
    tion Laws (United States), 139
National Health Service (Britain), 194
nationalism, 77, 95, 184–85
National Service Act (1941) (Britain),
    186
National Union of Societies for Equal
    Citizenship (Britain), 130
Nazi Germany. *See* fascism
Ndeunyema, Ndjodi, 69
neoliberalism, 202, 203
New Adelphi, 36

New Labour (Britain), 183
Newspeak, 64–68
New Statesman, 51–52
Nietzsche, Friedriech, 81
Nightwood (Barnes), 154
Nineteen Eighty-Four (Orwell)
    on abortion, 133
    on antisemitism, 50–51
    on censorship, 47, 52, 57
    on class, 126
    Cold War and, 41, 75
    common humanity in, 204–5
    Eastern European publication, 198
    on economic inequality, 103–4
    on fascism, 76
    gaslighting in, 60
    on imperialism, 13, 41, 87
    on intellectual silencing, 66
    Orwell's US reputation and, 196
    pessimism of, 194–95
    popularity of, 12, 16
    Russian views of, 77–79, 201
    sexual predation in, 145–47
    Spanish Civil War and, 40, 41, 51
    Stalinism and, 13, 41, 75, 194
    on thought control, 79–80
    title of, 80
    tragedy in, 135
    truth and, 43, 56, 91, 192
    ubiquitous potential for totalitari-
        anism and, 74
    See also invocations of Orwell
"Notes on Nationalism" (Orwell),
    77, 81
Notting Hill, 99–100, 101

Obama, Barack, 174
Obama, Michelle, 121
obfuscation, 63–65, 66, 80–81
Oliver, James, 54
Oliver, Jamie, 118, 119–20
opium trade, 23

Orwell, George
  Burma IPS service, 30, 31–34, 84,
    112–13
  censorship of, 44–47, 51–52, 57–58
  childhood and education of, 25–30,
    107–8, 109–10, 111
  as cultural product, 16
  current relevance of, 14–15, 16–17,
    76, 189, 192, 201
  death of, 194
  diet of, 118, 122
  on dying metaphors, 59
  Eastern European publication and,
    198
  family background of, 24–25
  humor and, 18–19
  Information Research Department
    list, 51, 52–55
  London and Paris sojourns, 34, 35,
    36, 113–14
  pen name of, 23, 34, 36
  on political writing, 61–63
  posthumous views of, 195–201
  relevance to 1960s Western society,
    198–99
  romances of, 35
  sexual predation by, 31, 155–59
  social awakening of, 35, 41–42, 102,
    112–13
  son's education, 174–75
  Spanish Civil War involvement,
    38–41, 44–46
  on truth vs. free speech, 43–44,
    51, 55
  unsuccessful marriage proposals by,
    29, 53, 155
Orwell, Sonia Browne (Orwell's wife),
    24
Orwell: The Life (Taylor), 157
Orwell: The New Life (Taylor), 157
Orwell and Empire (Kerr), 94, 150
Orwell Mystique, The (Patai), 132, 149

"Orwell's '1984' and Trump's America"
    (Gopnik), 12
Orwell's androcentrism, 14
  abortion and, 132–33, 134–38, 140,
    141–42
  childhood and, 26
  contemporary female views of,
    154–55
  portrayals of sexual predation and,
    145–54
  reform proposal limitations and,
    159–60
  in The Road to Wigan Pier, 126–27,
    129–30, 131
  sexual predation by Orwell, 31,
    155–59
  social awakening and, 35
  women's roles and, 187
Orwell's anti-imperialism
  absolute nature of, 73
  British left and, 86
  Burma IPS service and, 32–34, 36,
    84, 182
  costs of independence and, 87–88
  economic exploitation and, 85–87
  language and, 63
  Nineteen Eighty-Four and, 13, 41, 87
  Orwell's blueprint for socialist
    revolution and, 181–82
  postwar ambivalence about, 182
  sexual predation and, 150–51
  social awakening and, 35
  Streit's proposals and, 84–86
Orwell's blueprint for socialist revolu-
    tion, 161–92
  anti-imperialism and, 181–82
  class and, 163–64, 171
  Cold War and, 189–90
  common humanity and, 203–5
  current relevance of, 201–2
  economic inequality and, 164–65,
    166–68, 201–2

education and, 171–72, 174
House of Lords abolition and, 179
The Lion and the Unicorn on,
    162–63, 180
monarchy and, 179
nationalization and, 165, 166,
    167–68
neoliberalism and, 202, 203
Nineteen Eighty-Four as warning
    and, 194–95
optimism and, 193–94
rule of law and, 166, 167
social cohesion and, 168–70, 189,
    202–3
vagueness of, 161–62
violence and, 165–66
World War II and, 162–63, 164,
    165–66, 188–89
Orwell's Nose (Sutherland), 157
Orwell's Roses (Solnit), 94–95
Orwell's values
    antifascism, 12, 38, 184
    anti-totalitarianism, 15, 32, 40–41,
        45–46, 63
    Burma IPS service and, 32, 84,
        112–13
    critique of disinformation, 16, 40, 61
    on economic inequality, 103–4, 105,
        106–7
    patriotism, 29, 35, 94–97, 98, 163,
        204
    popular understandings of, 13–14,
        75–76, 198
    poverty and, 35
    racism and, 91–94, 181
    religion and, 81, 82–83
    secular humanism, 141
    social criticism, 35
    socialism, 13, 29, 37–38, 40, 63,
        95–96, 196–97
    See also Orwell's anti-imperialism;
        specific works

Orwell's works
    book reviews, 154
    A Clergyman's Daughter, 36,
        123–24, 151–52
    Coming Up for Air, 25, 36–37, 135,
        152–53
    "Eyewitness in Spain," 51
    "The Freedom of the Press," 44
    "A Hanging," 33, 92, 93, 203–4
    "How the Poor Die," 34
    "Inside the Whale," 37, 53, 162
    Keep the Aspidistra Flying, 36,
        134–38, 140, 141–42, 151
    The Lion and the Unicorn, 13,
        96–97, 162, 166, 179, 180, 182,
        204
    "My Country Right or Left," 29, 165
    "Notes on Nationalism," 77, 81
    "Politics and the English Language,"
        61–62
    "The Principles of Newspeak,"
        64–66
    "Shooting an Elephant," 18, 94
    "Socialism and Democracy," 165–66
    "Such, Such Were the Joys," 27–28,
        108
    "Why I Write," 62–63, 161
    "You and the Atom Bomb," 41
    *See also Animal Farm; Burmese
        Days; Down and Out in Paris and
        London; Homage to Catalonia;
        Nineteen Eighty-Four; Road to
        Wigan Pier, The*

Paine, Thomas, 163
Paltrow, Gwyneth, 118–19
Partisan Review, 55
Patai, Daphne, 132, 149
patriarchy, 129–60
    bodily autonomy and, 132–33, 153
    COVID-19 pandemic and, 188
    curriculum conflicts and, 67

patriarchy (*continued*)
  economic inequality and, 166–67
  persistence of, 14, 131, 193
  socialism and, 129, 131, 144–45
  World War II and, 185–87
  See also abortion; Orwell's andro-
    centrism; sexual predation
patriotism, 29, 35, 94–97, 98, 163, 204
Phillips, William, 55
Picasso, Pablo, 38
Piketty, Thomas, 100–101, 102,
  167–68, 201–2
Pinsker, Joe, 201–2
Planned Parenthood (United States),
  134, 139
Polanski, Roman, 159
"Politics and the English Language"
  (Orwell), 61–62
Popular Front (Britain), 46
POUM (Partido Obrero de Unifi-
    cación Marxista) (Workers' Party
    of Marxist Unification) (Spain),
    40–41, 45, 52
Poverty, by America (Desmond), 201
poverty, 35, 104, 112–13, 201
  See also class; economic inequality
"Principles of Newspeak, The"
  (Orwell), 64–66
Pritchett, V. S., 32, 114
propaganda, 16
Putin, Vladimir, 12, 66, 97, 193
  See also Ukraine War

quietism, 36–37, 162

Rachman, Peter, 125
racism
  bodily autonomy and, 134
  book bans and, 68
  curriculum conflicts and, 67, 71–72
  economic inequality and, 88–89
  Nazi antisemitism and, 81

Orwell's values and, 91–94, 181
persistence of, 72–73
slavery reparations movement and,
  89–90
"white man's burden" and, 181, 182
Rahv, Philip, 55
Rashford, Marcus, 176, 178
Reagan, Ronald, 199
Rees, Richard, 36
Reeves, Richard, 111–12
religion, 81–83, 109
reparations
  for enslavement, 89–90
  for imperialism, 90–91, 182–83,
    184–85
Rhodes, Cecil, 69
Road to Serfdom, A (Hayek), 190
Road to Wigan Pier, The (Orwell)
  androcentrism in, 126–27, 129–30,
    131
  on class, 28, 114–15, 116–18, 120,
    171
  common humanity in, 204
  on credit, 123
  current relevance of, 201
  on feminism, 129–30
  on housing, 124
  on imperialism, 73, 86
  Orwell's blueprint for socialist
    revolution and, 162
  Orwell's reputation and, 40
  on Orwell's social awakening,
    112–13
  publication of, 46
  on racism, 89
  on socialism, 37–38
  US reputation and, 196
Robinson, Calvin, 71
Rodden, John, 16
Roe v. Wade, 133, 134, 139
Rosie the Riveter, 185–86
Rudenko, Anastasia, 78

Russell, Bertrand, 103
Russia
    authoritarianism in, 193
    views of *Nineteen Eighty-Four*,
        77–79, 201
    See also Ukraine war

Salkeld, Brenda, 155, 157
Sanchez, Pedro, 170–71
Sanders, Bernie, 131
Satia, Priya, 72
Schama, Simon, 68
sexism. *See* patriarchy
sexual predation, 145–54
    in *Burmese Days*, 150–51
    "cancel culture" and, 158–59
    on *Coming Up for Air*, 152–53
    current debates on, 145
    in *Down and Out in Paris and
        London*, 147–50, 151, 152
    in *Keep the Aspidistra Flying*, 151
    #MeToo movement and, 59, 133,
        155
    in *Nineteen Eighty-Four*, 145–47
    by Orwell, 31, 155–59
shadow banning, 49
"Shooting an Elephant" (Orwell), 18,
    94
Silin, Dmitry, 78
social cohesion, 168–70, 189, 202–3
Social Gospel movement, 109
socialism
    abortion and, 140–41
    COVID-19 pandemic and, 170
    economic inequality and, 102–3,
        104
    fin de siècle birth of, 109
    free speech and, 193
    language and, 63
    Marx and, 196–97
    Orwell's belief in, 13, 29, 38, 40, 63,
        95–96, 196–97

    Orwell's patriotism and, 29, 95–96,
        163
    patriarchy and, 129, 131, 144–45
    POUM and, 40
    The Road to Wigan Pier on, 37–38
    See also Orwell's blueprint for
        socialist revolution
"Socialism and Democracy" (Orwell),
    165–66
Socialist Party (France), 109
Socialist Party of America, 109
Socialist Patriot, The (Stansky), 163
Socialist Workers Party (Britain), 131
Solnit, Rebecca, 94–95
Sotomayor, Sonia, 11–12
South Riding (Holtby), 153–54
Soviet Union
    abortion and, 140
    banning of *Nineteen Eighty-Four*, 78
    British left support for, 46, 53, 64,
        194
    doublethink and, 199
    nationalization and, 165
    religion in, 81–82
    Spanish Civil War and, 39, 40, 45,
        52
    World War II and, 47
    See also Cold War; Stalinism
Spanish Civil War, 84
    British left and, 46, 58
    censorship of Orwell and, 44–47,
        51–52, 57, 58–59
    Orwell's involvement in, 38–41,
        44–46
    social cohesion and, 202–3
    See also Homage to Catalonia
Spanish Cockpit, The (Borkenau), 51–52
Stalinism
    Animal Farm and, 13, 41, 103, 106,
        194
    antisemitism and, 51
    British left and, 64

Spanish Civil War (*continued*)
    language and, 63
    Nineteen Eighty-Four and, 13, 41,
        75, 194
    Orwell's US reputation and, 196
    religion and, 81–82
    Spanish Civil War and, 40–41, 45
Stansky, Peter, 28–29, 163
Starmer, Keir, 17
Stopes, Marie, 131
Strachey, John, 174–75
Strange World, 67
Streit, Clarence, 84–86
"Such, Such Were the Joys" (Orwell),
    27–28, 108
Summerskill, Edith, 131
Sunak, Rishi, 170, 172
Sutherland, John, 157
Swayne, Desmond, 177

Taylor, D. J., 157
Their Eyes Were Watching God (Hur-
    ston), 154
thought control, 79–80
303 Creative LLC v. Elenis, 11–12
Time & Tide, 130
Time for Socialism (Piketty), 102–3
Topp, Sylvia, 186
totalitarianism
    antisemitism and, 51
    Orwell's opposition to, 15, 32,
        40–41, 45–46, 63
    thought control and, 79–80
    ubiquitous potential for, 74, 77
Traverso, Enzo, 71
Trump, Donald, 12, 47–48, 90, 169,
    170, 183
Trump, Donald, Jr., 47, 51, 75–76
truth
    vs. alternative facts, 56
    censorship and, 55, 56–57
    vs. free speech, 43–44, 51, 55–57, 62

history and, 69, 91, 192
Orwell's anti-imperialism and, 85,
    86
See also disinformation; language
Truth Social, 48
Tselovalnikova, Darya, 78–79
Twitter (X), 47–50, 57
Two-Income Trap, The (Warren and
    Tyagi), 110
Tyagi, Amelia Warren, 110

Ukraine war, 12, 38–39, 66, 97–98, 201
United Nations, 184
Uyghur Muslims, 80–81

vaccine nationalism, 184–85
Venables, Dione, 155–56
Vietnam War, 199

Warren, Elizabeth, 110
"White Man's Burden" (Kipling), 181
"Why I Write" (Orwell), 62–63, 161
Why Orwell Matters (Hitchens), 131
Wifedom (Funder), 158
Wigan Pier Revisited (Campbell), 126
Wilkinson, Ellen, 86, 153, 186–87
working class. *See* class
World War I, 28–29, 30, 38
World War II
    COVID-19 pandemic invocations,
        168–70
    disinformation and, 55–56
    imperialism and, 86, 180–81, 184
    Nazi-Soviet pact, 47
    Orwell's blueprint for socialist revo-
        lution and, 162–63, 164, 165–66,
        188–89
    Orwell's Home Guard service, 95
    patriarchy and, 185–87
    Russian Orthodox Church and, 82

Xi Jinping, 80, 81, 193, 200